amigurume eats

MAKE CUTE SCENTED
CROCHET FOODS

amigurume

eats

Allison Hoffman

LARK
New York

New York

An Imprint of Sterling Publishing Co., Inc.
1166 Avenue of the Americas
New York, NY 10036

ISBN 978-1-4547-1071-4

Distributed in Canada by Sterling Publishing Co., Inc.
c/o Canadian Manda Group, 664 Annette Street
Toronto, Ontario, M6S 2C8, Canada
Distributed in the United Kingdom by GMC Distribution Services
Castle Place, 166 High Street, Lewes, East Sussex, BN7 1XU, England
Distributed in Australia by NewSouth Books
University of New South Wales, Sydney, NSW 2052, Australia

For information about custom editions, special sales, and premium and corporate purchases,
please contact Sterling Special Sales at 800-805-5489 or specialsales@sterlingpublishing.com.

Manufactured in China

2 4 6 8 10 9 7 5 3 1

larkcrafts.com
sterlingpublishing.com

Cover and interior design by Shannon Nicole Plunkett
Photography by Christopher Bain

contents

INTRODUCTION

You're five years old and sitting at the dinner table. Your favorite foods are on your plate, the scents wafting up your five-year-old nose. Your five-year-old hands fidget in your lap, but you don't know how long you can stand it. Finally, you reach out and grab for something, anything, and you're (gasp!) playing with your food!

Yep, we've all done it. Kids can't keep their hands out of their meals. Even adults can get messy when eating ice cream or saucy stuff. (I'm not eating a delicious slice of cheesy New York–style pizza with a fork, thank you very much!) What if there was a way you could play with your food without having to wash your hands? Good news! The fun, crocheted AmiguruME Eats in this book are scented and soft, fun to play with, and easy to make.

For my first two books, *AmiguruME* and *AmiguruME Pets*, I loved making things that were both fun to look at and fun to make. I wanted to complement these patterns with more projects that would flex my creative muscles, so I thought about other items that people love to crochet. I knew crocheted food was popular, but I wanted to make my versions a little different and keep them in line with the super-cute AmiguruME style. When I was a kid, I lived for scratch-and-sniff stickers. Just the promise of a scented sticker on the top of my perfect spelling test was enough for me to memorize those spelling words backwards and forwards. What if you could squeeze your crocheted food and release the scent of real food? I soon discovered that it's easy to give food amigurumi that same scratch-and-sniff thrill with a handful of spices or a few drops of scented oil. Scents make the food all the more realistic, and you don't have to even study! And because I'm a sucker for anything with a cute little face, lots of these foods smile at me just like the people and pets in my previous books did.

We'll start with the basics. If you've never crocheted before, you can learn in the How to Crochet section. In the Tools and Materials sections, I explain exactly what you'll need to make fun food and scented treats.

Starting with Breakfast, you'll learn how to make savory eggs and bacon and sweet waffles and pancakes to tide you over until Lunch. Crochet a sandwich and a bag of chips, but save room for Dinner. After you've finished your crocheted steak and salad, end with a dessert from the Sweet Treats section, perhaps cake or ice cream. As you make your way through each featured meal and snack, you'll find tips on how to customize your AmiguruME Eats. Many projects recommend garnishes, toppings, sauces, and more, so your food will look uniquely delicious. To make your AmiguruME Eats even more realistic, crochet cool stuff from the Extras section, like plates, utensils, or even a lunch box that opens and closes.

There are so many fun things to do with AmiguruME Eats. Make a set of decorative crocheted food to display in your home. Crochet a special meal to celebrate a birthday. Make scented treats for unique gifts. I hope you're inspired and hungry by the time you finish reading this book. Now dig in!

getting started

Basic tools and some fun yarn are all you'll need to create any food you can think of! No hard-to-find ingredients or obscure spices are needed to cook up these yarn-based treats.

TOOLS

Crochet Hooks

For amigurumi like the foods you'll make in this book, I like to use a smaller-than-average hook. Using a small hook makes a tight fabric and prevents stuffing from coming through any loose holes. In the patterns, the hooks are given in U.S. sizes with their metric equivalents.

My favorite hooks are the ones with ergonomic handles. Because of the small detail work involved in many of the patterns, you'll probably also enjoy using a crochet hook that is comfortable to use on small stitches. If you prefer using a larger hook, feel free to do so. Your foods might be a little larger than the ones shown, but they will come out just fine as long as the crocheted fabric is dense and does not have large spaces between the stitches.

Needles

You'll need a yarn needle and, for some of the AmiguruME Eats patterns, an embroidery needle. A yarn needle has a blunter tip than a sewing needle, which enables it to move easily in and out of crocheted fabric without splitting yarn. Some have a bent tip, which makes them easy to use when you stitch into the surface of your crocheted foods, finish up and weave in ends, or assemble the pieces of your projects. An embroidery needle is used with embroidery floss to add details, like decorations, mouths, or words on labels.

Scissors

A good pair of sharp scissors is absolutely necessary. You'll be snipping yarn and embroidery floss, as well as felt details.

Glue

High-quality craft glue will work wonders for attaching tiny bits of felt if you don't want to stitch them on. A strong cyanoacrylate glue in a gel formula also makes quick work of tiny details.

Other Tools

A long dowel or even a knitting needle will do the trick for stuffing your crocheted foods. Stitch markers are indispensable for keeping track of the spiral rounds used in amigurumi. You need locking stitch markers, so you can mark the start of a round of stitches, for example, and then move the marker up when you start the next round. A safety pin or a small piece of pipe cleaner can serve as a homemade stitch marker, or they can be bought in a variety of styles.

MATERIALS

Yarn

One convenient thing about amigurumi is that it is so easy to find the yarn you need to use at an affordable price. You might look for the fanciest yarns made of only the best fibers for crocheted clothing items, but you can use any type for these projects. Acrylic, cotton, or wool—anything goes, as long as the yarn can be crocheted to form a dense fabric.

Amigurumi benefits from the structure and stitch definition a simple worsted weight yarn provides. Not only is worsted weight yarn available everywhere, its also available in an endless supply of colors. Worsted weight yarn, when used with a smaller hook than the yarn label usually calls for, makes a strong and sturdy fabric. When you're making amigurumi, this yarn-to-tiny hook ratio is very important, because it means the stuffing won't seep out of your creations.

Some of the patterns in AmiguruME Eats benefit from a finer yarn than worsted, like a sport weight. Why the switch? I like to use a finer gauge yarn for items that need a lot of detail, like splashes of syrup, tiny slices of lemon, and swirls of frosting. Keep your stitches tight for these items too.

Stuffing

Most of the foods you will crochet will need to be stuffed. Polyester fiberfill is the most readily available material and also your best option. It stays fluffy and resists clumping, unlike some natural fibers.

Safety Eyes (Optional)

For food with a little personality, tiny safety eyes add a cute touch! Before closing up your work, insert the eyes according to the package directions. I like plain black 5-mm ones, but feel free to use whatever color and size you think looks the best.

Felt

Some crocheted foods need labels or extra decoration. In these instances, felt adds just the right finishing touch. Cut out letters, faces, or shapes, and sew or glue them onto your foods. Wool felt is an option, but you're more likely to find polyester felt in every color and pattern you can dream of at your local craft store.

Embroidery Floss

You'll need embroidery floss for adding smiles, texture, or words to your food. Use your embroidery needle, the full six strands of floss (don't split it), and stitch right onto the surface of your crocheted food. I always have at least half a dozen skeins of black embroidery floss in my desk drawer, but I keep a basic rainbow of colors on hand too.

Permanent Markers

Yes, I'm asking you to get some permanent markers and draw on your crocheted objects! I know, it's a scary proposition, but trust me. Some details look great with a few swipes of a marker. Do you want a crocheted steak with realistic grill marks or a slice of toast with a smear of grape jelly? Use permanent marker. You'll definitely be impressed with the results. Basic colors like brown, black, red, and purple should be enough to get started. See the project list of materials for specifics.

Plastic Canvas Sheets

Plastic canvas is such a versatile product. It's flexible yet sturdy and easy to cut into any size or shape you need. In this book, I use it to line a lunch box, form the base of a plate, and make handles for utensils, among other things. Look for a rigid, heavier weight plastic canvas. Very flexible and lightweight varieties won't hold their shape as well.

Other Materials

Tiny colorful pompoms and small beads make great "cereal" or "sprinkles," and eyeshadow or colored chalk adds subtle shading or color to your foods. D-rings are useful for attaching handles on a lunch box, and you can sometimes use card stock interchangeably with plastic canvas, especially on very small projects. You might even find your own fun supplies to use in your AmiguruME Eats. I love browsing around the craft store, finding random odds and ends to repurpose in my work.

Scents

Make your crocheted food stand out with scents! What better way to evoke memories or good feelings than with the sense of smell? There are several ways to scent your AmiguruME Eats. The options are listed below in order based on scent strength, from strongest to more subtle.

Oils and Extracts

For scents like vanilla, root beer, and maple, there are strongly scented extracts that work great for crocheted toys. Essential oils and fragrance oils used in oil warmers or reed diffusers work well too. Just a few drops of oil or extract will give you a strong, long-lasting scent.

Wax Melts

Scented wax melts are extremely popular home fragrance products. Luckily for us, there are tons of options available in stores, and homemade versions (in some wildly unique scents) are all over the Internet. Looking for pizza-scented or ramen noodle–scented wax? Or would you rather play it safe with birthday cake

or cinnamon donut? Small chunks of wax melt can be broken off and inserted directly into your creations, or you can use fabric or cheesecloth to contain the pieces. Some wax melts come in tiny beads. No matter what form, wax scents last a long time and are usually scented strongly.

Dry Spices, Mixes, and Foods

There are a few simple rules to follow when scenting your crocheted toys with edible items. Do not use anything that is perishable. If you have to keep it refrigerated, it doesn't belong in your amigurumi. Anything that would attract pests also isn't recommended. Most important, and say this with me: "If in doubt, leave it out." (For extra help, you can use the handy Scent Cheat Sheet on pages 6–7.) I love making cheesecloth or fabric sachets out of dried herbs and ground spices (page 22). Not only do they smell amazing, they won't attract bugs or make a mess. Tea bags are almost ready-made for AmiguruME Eats. In addition to black tea and green tea, you'll find a huge variety of fruit and herbal teas that are perfect for use in crocheted fruits and desserts.

Scent Cheat Sheet

SCENT	EXTRACT	ESSENTIAL/ FRAGRANCE OIL	WAX MELT	SPICES/ SEASONINGS	FOOD ITEMS
Apple		X	X	Apple pie spice	
Bacon			X	Bacon-flavored salt	
Banana		X	X		
Berry		X	X		Berry tea bag
Blueberry		X	X		Blueberry tea bag
Bread			X		
Buffalo wings				Buffalo wing seasoning mix	
Butter					Butter-flavored granules
Cheese					Cheese-flavored seasoning
Cherry		X	X		Cherry drink mix
Chocolate			X	Cocoa powder	
Cinnamon		X	X	Cinnamon	
Coconut	X	X	X		
Coffee			X		Coffee beans
Cola		X			
Dill				Dried dill	
French Fries				French fry seasoning	
Grape					Grape drink mix
Guacamole				Guacamole seasoning	

SCENT	EXTRACT	ESSENTIAL/ FRAGRANCE OIL	WAX MELT	SPICES/ SEASONINGS	FOOD ITEMS
Lemon/ Lime	X	X	X		Lemonade/ limeade drink mix
Maple	X		X		
Mint	X	X	X		
Mustard				Dried mustard powder	
Orange	X	X	X		Orange drink mix
Peanut Butter			X		Peanut butter powder
Pizza				Italian seasoning or dried basil or oregano	
Poultry				Poultry seasoning	
Ranch				Ranch dressing mix	
Root Beer	X				
Rye Bread				Rye seeds	
Spaghetti				Italian seasoning mix or dried basil	
Steak				Steak seasoning	
Strawberry		X	X		Strawberry drink mix
Taco				Taco seasoning mix	
Tea					Tea bag
Vanilla	X	X	X		

HOW TO CROCHET

Before you can start making delectable crocheted food, you need to learn a couple of basics. If you already know how to crochet, you can move on and get started with a project. If you need to find your bearings, read on!

Luckily for you, amigurumi is made using really simple stitches and techniques. Once you learn these simple building blocks, you'll be able to make a smorgasbord of crocheted treats.

Hold Your Hook

There are many ways people hold their crochet hooks. The two basic grips are the pencil grip and the overhand grip. Try out both and see which is most comfortable to you. It is hard to switch to a different

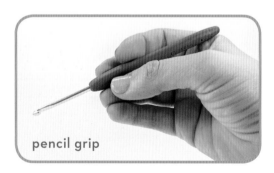

pencil grip

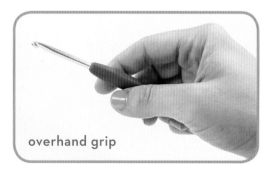

overhand grip

grip once you've found your favorite. I use the pencil grip.

Now that you've got a hold on your hook, try out some basic stitches. You've got to figure out how to handle the yarn, which for some people presents a challenge at first. Stay with it—you've got this!

Handling Yarn

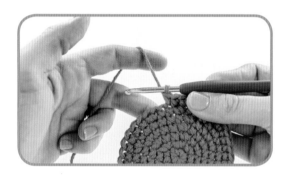

When you crochet, your hook goes in your dominant hand (are you a righty or a lefty?), and the yarn goes in the other hand. (The photos show a right-handed person working.) Some people like to intricately wrap the yarn around their fingers to provide the tension that is necessary for even stitches, and some people just let the yarn fall gently over their hands. Whatever is comfortable to you is the right way to do it.

As you work crochet stitches, keep in mind that every time you move the yarn around the hook, referred to as a "yarn over" or "yo," you will wrap the yarn from the back to the front of the hook.

Chain Stitch (ch)

The chain stitch is used as a foundation stitch for crocheting, especially when crocheting something flat in rows. It is also used at the end of rows for turning.

1. To make a chain stitch, begin with a slip knot on your hook (A, B, C). This knot does not count as a stitch, but simply holds the yarn onto your hook for you to do the first stitch.

2. Holding your hook in one hand (your working hand) and the yarn coming from the ball in the other hand, bring the yarn over the hook (yarn over). It will look like there are two loops of yarn lying over the top of your hook (D).

3. Catch the yarn that you just wrapped with the hook and pull it through the first loop on your hook. One loop will remain on your hook, and you've just completed one chain stitch (E). Repeat steps 2 and 3 for as many chain stitches as the pattern calls for (F).

Each stitch will be a "v" shape. Keep that in mind as you start counting your stitches. The slip knot we started with will not look like a "v" and is not counted as a stitch. The chain stitch will have a "v" on the front and a little bump on the back. When you start crocheting into a chain, your goal will be to insert your hook between the "v" on top and the bump on the back. This is challenging, even for experienced crocheters, and many people (ahem!) cheat a little and insert the hook into the middle of the v for that first row of stitches, or even into the back bar or bump of the chain. This leaves a nice lower edge. Try it several ways and see what is most comfortable for you.

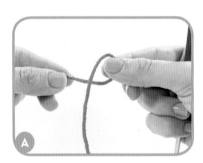

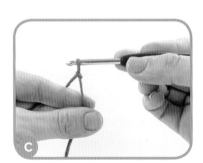

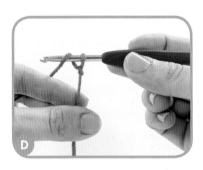

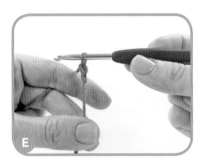

Slip Stitch (sl st)

The slip stitch in crochet is mainly used to move around your work without adding much height to your crocheted piece. It can also be used to join rounds in circular crochet. Because we will be using the Adjustable Ring method for crocheting in the round, which you'll learn later, the slip stitch will be used mainly for fastening off work.

1. Insert the hook into the next stitch. Catch the yarn, without first wrapping a loop around your hook, and pull up a loop.

2. Pull the loop all the way through the loop on your hook. You are left with one loop on your hook, and one slip stitch has been made.

Single Crochet (sc)

There's a basic stitch that you'll use every time you make a project in this book: the single crochet. It is short and sturdy, so for amigurumi it is perfect for making a dense fabric. All the other stitches you'll learn are variations on the single crochet. The instructions here address crocheting into stitches. Of course when you start, you will crochet into a chain (for rows in flat projects) or a ring (for rounds in projects that are worked in the round). Practice the single crochet stitch until you've mastered it, and all of the other stitches to follow will come easily.

1. Insert your hook into the front of the fabric (or chain), under both loops of the stitch (or chain) (A),

and pull a loop through to the front. Two loops will be on your hook (B).

2. Wrap the working yarn around your hook. There will be three loops on your hook (C). Pull the last loop through the first two loops. Only one loop will remain on the hook. This is one single crochet stitch (D).

Reverse Single Crochet (reverse sc)

The reverse single crochet stitch is just that. You are working a single crochet in the opposite direction than it is normally worked. It feels really strange the first time you make this stitch, but the results are worth it. A round of reverse single crochet gives a finished and sturdy edge to your work.

1. Insert your hook from the front into the back of the fabric (or chain), under both loops of the next stitch to the right (A). Wrap the working yarn around your hook and pull up a loop through the back. Two loops will be on your hook (B).

2. Yarn over. There will be three loops on your hook (C). Pull the yarn through the first two loops on the hook. There will be one loop on your hook. You have completed a reverse single crochet stitch (D).

Adjustable Ring Method

Making an adjustable ring only requires a few extra steps and will give your in-the-round projects a smooth start. There are alternative ways to start crocheting in the round, but these other methods leave tiny holes. The chain stitch you just learned will be used only once, in the very beginning, but is a key element.

1. Begin by making a small ring or loop with the yarn, crossing the end of the yarn over the front of the working yarn and leaving a 6-inch (15 cm) tail (A). This ring will be closed in the last step.

2. Hold where both strands of yarn overlap along the ring, keeping the working yarn behind the ring. Moving from front to back, insert your crochet hook into

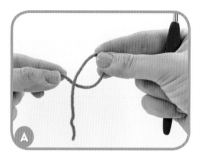

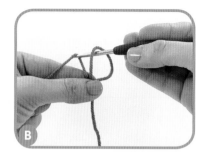

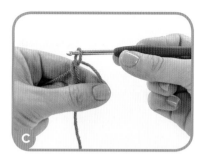

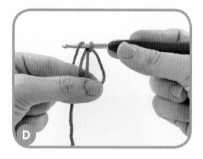

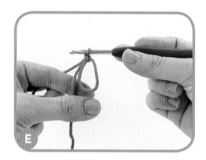

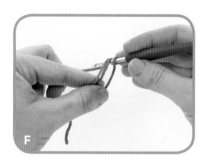

the ring (B), and pull up a loop from the working yarn (C). Make one chain stitch (ch) by yarning over from back to front and pulling it through the loop on your hook (D). There will be one loop on your hook (E).

3. Insert your crochet hook back into the ring (F). Pull a loop of working yarn through the center of the ring (G).

4. Now there are two loops on your crochet hook. Yarn over (H) and pull through both

loops, completing a single crochet stitch (sc) (I).

5. Continue crocheting around both the tail and the ring, repeating steps 3 and 4, until you have the desired number of single crochet stitches (J). When you do, gently pull on the yarn tail to close up the ring. The ring of stitches you have just created will be the base for all of the rest of your stitches and counts as the first round.

Half Double Crochet (hdc)

Half double crochet stitches are exactly what they imply. They are half of a double crochet stitch, which you'll learn next. They are a little taller than a single crochet.

1. Before inserting your hook under the stitch, yarn over (A). Continue on as if you were going to make a single crochet. Insert your hook under the "v" of the next stitch (B) and pull up a loop. Now you will have three loops on your hook (C).

2. Wrap the working yarn around your hook (D). There will be four loops on your hook. Pull the last loop through the first three loops. Only one loop will remain on the hook (E). This completes one half double crochet stitch.

Double Crochet (dc)

Double crochet stitches are twice as tall as single crochet stitches.

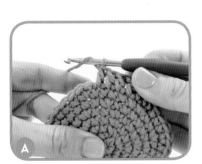 

1. Wrap the yarn around the hook (yarn over) (A) and insert your hook into the next stitch (B). Pull up a loop. Three loops will be on your hook (C).

2. Yarn over (D) and pull the yarn through the first two loops on the hook. Two loops will remain on the hook (E).

3. Yarn over again (F) and pull the yarn through the last two loops on the hook. There will be one loop on the hook (G). One double crochet stitch has been made.

Treble Crochet (tr)

The treble crochet stitch is the tallest stitch you'll use in this book.

1. Wrap the yarn around the hook twice (yarn over twice) (A) and insert your hook into the next stitch (B). Pull up a loop. Four loops will be on your hook (C).

2. Yarn over (D) and pull the yarn through the first two loops on the hook. Three loops will be on the hook (E).

3. Yarn over again (F) and pull the yarn through the first two loops on the hook. Two loops will be on the hook (G).

4. Yarn over one last time (H) and pull the yarn through the last two loops on the hook. You have made one treble crochet stitch (I).

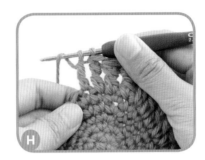

Bobble Stitch

The bobble stitch is used for texture in your AmiguruME Eats like the Pickle, page 58, and the Pie, page 110. It creates a small round bump in your work using several double crochets. You will see this in patterns written like this: bobble [5 dc]. The number indicates how many double crochets you need to make the bobble stitch.

1. Yarn over (A) and insert the hook into the next stitch (B). Pull up a loop (C). Three loops will be on the hook.

2. Yarn over (D) and pull the yarn through just two

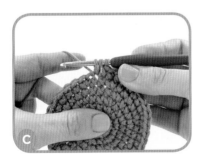

loops. Two loops will remain on your hook (E).

3. Repeat steps 1 and 2 into the same stitch (F) until you've made the number of double crochets that was indicated in the brackets. Each time step 2 is completed, there will be one more loop on your hook. When you've made the required number of double crochets, the number of loops on your hook will be one more than the number of double crochets you made. For example, if the pattern calls for bobble [5 dc], you will have six loops on your hook (G).

4. Yarn over (H) and pull through all the loops on your hook. One loop remains on your hook, and you've made one bobble stitch (I).

5. When you crochet into the next stitch, the bobble stitch you just made will puff out (J). You may need to help the bobble puff out to the right side of the fabric by gently pushing it to the outside.

Front Post Double Crochet (FPdc)

Lots of people are intimidated by post stitches in crochet. Instead of working into the top of the stitch, you work

around its post, the vertical part that links the double crochet stitch with the stitch below it. While it does look a little tricky,

this fun stitch adds lots of texture to your cro-cheted food.

1. Yarn over (A). Insert your hook from the front of the fabric to the back, behind the post of the next stitch, and bring the hook out through the front of the fabric on the other side of the post (B). Yarn over and pull up a loop behind the post. There will be three loops on your hook (C).

2. Yarn over (D) and draw the yarn through the first two loops on your hook. There will be two loops on your hook (E).

3. Yarn over again (F) and pull the yarn through the remaining two loops on your hook. One front post double crochet stitch has been made (G).

Crocheting into Chain Spaces (ch-sp)

Sometimes you will be crocheting into a chain space, which is a gap made up of one or more chain stitches (A). Instead of cro-cheting into the front and back loops of these chain stitches, you will insert your hook into the space in your fabric (B). You will then complete the stitch as you normally would.

In the patterns, like the one for the Lunch Box (page 124), chain spaces will be written like this: ch-2 sp. The number indicates how many chain stitches are used to make the chain space. For rows that contain chain spaces, the number of chain spaces will be listed after the stitch count.

Increasing

Increasing in crochet is very simple. You will crochet two stitches into one stitch. Increases in rounds are spaced evenly, as written in each pattern. Try staggering the increases so that the finished piece will have a rounder shape.

For example, crocheting a few stitches before beginning an increase repeat will make the increase blend in easily, while stacking the increases, or increasing in the same spot in each round, is more noticeable.

Decreasing

To decrease, you have a couple of options, as described here.

Single Crochet Two Together (sc2tog)

You may single crochet two stitches together by inserting your hook into the next stitch (A), pulling up a loop (B), inserting into the next stitch after that (C) and pulling up another loop (D), and then yarning over (E) and pulling the loop through all the loops on your hook. One loop remains and you have created one sc2tog decrease (F). This is the traditional method used, but it may leave tiny gaps before and after the stitch. When working in rows, I like to use the sc2tog decrease.

Half Double Crochet Two Together (hdc2tog)

When you're working with tall half double crochet stitches, you'll need a decrease that is the same height. Yarn over (A), insert your hook into the next stitch (B), and pull up a loop. Three loops will be on your hook (C). Yarn over (D), then insert hook into next stitch (E), and pull up a loop. Five loops will be on your hook (F). Yarn over one last time (G) and pull through all the loops on your hook, combining the two stitches and decreasing (H).

Crocheting into Back Loops Only (BLO) or Front Loops Only (FLO)

In most instances, each stitch is crocheted under both loops of the stitch in the previous row or round. Sometimes it's necessary to crochet into only one loop of the stitch. This creates a little ridge on the front or back of the work, depending on which loop you crochet into, and makes a stretchier and somewhat thinner fabric. When a pattern calls for crocheting into the back loops only, or BLO, you will insert your hook into the middle of the "v" of the stitch (A), under only the back of the stitch. If the pattern tells you to crochet into the front loops only, or FLO, you will insert your hook into the front of the stitch, under only the front loop, and out through the middle of the "v" (B).

Changing Color

There will come a time when you're crocheting that you will want to change colors, or you may run out of yarn and need to add yarn from a new ball. It is quite simple to perform a quick change without making a single knot.

1. Work the last stitch before the change until the last step of the stitch, just before your last yarn over.

2. Instead of finishing the stitch with the old yarn, drop it to the back and yarn over with the new color (A); pull a loop of the new yarn through the remaining loops on the hook (B). Continue to the next stitch with the new yarn (C).

3. To secure the two ends, continue crocheting, laying the yarn tails on top of the stitches and crocheting over them several times. Clip the tails, leaving several inches of length. After finishing the piece you are working on, you can weave in the ends with a yarn needle.

Fastening Off

All done? Time to fasten off.

Simply finish your last stitch, cut the yarn about 6 inches (15 cm) away from the stitch, and hook the strand, pulling it all the way through the loop on your hook.

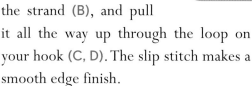

When working in the round, after completing your final stitch, make a slip stitch (sl st): insert your hook into the next stitch (A), hook the strand (B), and pull it all the way up through the loop on your hook (C, D). The slip stitch makes a smooth edge finish.

Finish by weaving in the yarn tail with a yarn needle. For stuffed toys, the yarn end can be hidden inside the toy. Insert the needle into the toy all the way through to the other side, pulling tightly. Clip the yarn tail close to the surface, and let go, and the yarn tail will retract, hiding itself inside.

Special Amigurumi Techniques

There are several noncrochet techniques you'll need to learn that are unique to making amigurumi.

months for all of my amigurumi needs. You can use a knitting needle or narrow dowel to stuff your creations.

Stuff It

With the exception of flat items, like the Bacon (page 28) and Cookies (page 116), almost all of your AmiguruME Eats will need to be stuffed. With AmiguruME people and pets, I recommended stuffing until you can't stuff anymore. Because crocheted foods need to maintain structure and form, add just a little at a time until your item takes shape. You can buy bags of polyester or cotton stuffing at most discount or craft big box stores. I buy a huge box every few

Construct It

When you're crocheting foods with small pieces that need to be sewn together, you'll need to follow these easy instructions.

Use long straight pins to hold the pieces together; then sew the parts together with matching yarn and a yarn needle. Many times the stitches will line right up and you can sew stitch to stitch, creating a seamless join. Most of the time, however, you're going to need to sew as discreetly as possible, up through one piece, out, back down through the other piece, out, and so on. Try not to split the yarn; sew between stitches instead of through them. When you're finished, you can pull the yarn tight, knot it close to the surface, let the knot retract back inside, and then weave the yarn tail back out through another spot. This will hide the knot inside and redirect the yarn tail from coming out in the same spot.

Scent It

Here's where the fun begins. Scenting your crocheted food lends a new twist that you or the recipient of your handiwork might not expect!

If you are using whole spices, dried herbs, or foods like coffee beans, the best way to include them in crocheted food is to make a square sachet with two layers of cheesecloth. Insert the spices, herbs, or food into the square (a teaspoon or two should be enough) and tie the corners together with a

scrap of yarn. Stuff the little sachet into your crocheted food. Tea bags make scenting your AmiguruME Eats even easier. Because a tea bag is a sachet, just insert it into your work when you're stuffing.

If you are using ground spices or fine powders (like cinnamon, cocoa powder, chili powder, drink mix, or dried seasoning blends), the loose weave of cheesecloth might not contain them. In these cases, construct a flat sachet from a scrap of fabric. Fold the fabric in half and sew the edges to make a pocket, insert your finely ground scent, and sew the remaining edge closed. Insert the sachet into your crocheted foods.

For extracts and essential oils, simply apply a few drops to a cotton ball, and then insert it into a cheesecloth sachet. If the sachet feels moist, wait for it to dry before inserting into your crocheted items. The scent will remain strong even after it has dried.

For wax melts, you can either insert the chunks of wax directly into your crocheted items when you're stuffing them, or you can make sachets. Sachets are especially useful if you are using small wax beads or if you've broken up the wax melt into tiny pieces, which you probably want to do if you're scenting something small.

Adding Faces

If you're smiling when you eat an ice cream cone (and I know you are), then shouldn't your ice cream cone be able to smile back? Adding cute little faces to your crocheted foods is totally optional, but I love how they bring these little guys to life.

For items that are this small, I use tiny eyes. This way, you can make the face in scale with the food, giving your little AmiguruME Eats a diminutive expression. I usually like to add eyes to the lower third of the front of the food to make the face look even tinier. For the mouth, I use the full six strands of black embroidery floss (feel free to use pink or red) and stitch a tiny loose "v" shape that is centered just below the eyes. Don't feel like your food has to smile. After all, a cookie with a bite taken out of it or a baked fish that has met his sad fate might not necessarily be smiling! A frown would be made the same way, but with an upside-down "v."

Add a face when you have a full surface to work on so that you can position the face as you'd like. Make sure you have an opening to the inside of your work so you can properly attach the eyes. Alternatively, you can wait until you're completely done to add a face. I like to do this if I'm not quite sure where I want the face to go. Add a little drop of cyanoacrylate glue to the post of each eye and push it into the amigurumi. Allow it to fully dry before handling, and then stitch the mouth onto the surface.

EMBROIDERY HOW-TO

When you're finished crocheting your amigurumi, you'll want to add some embroidery for texture, labels, or other details. A few stitches are all you need for some interesting and effective details.

straight stitch

For simple short lines or other disconnected stitches, use a straight stitch of any length.

back stitch

For a thin outline, use back stitch. The stitches are small and even. Working from right to left, make a short stitch. Pull the needle back up a stitch ahead, and then insert it back down at the beginning of the first stitch. Continue working from right to left, connecting stitches, until you make a line of the desired length.

cross-stitch

The beautiful thing about working in single crochet is that each stitch is a perfect square. This gives you the perfect canvas for making any small design with these x-shaped stitches. Pull the needle up through the lower right corner of a crochet stitch, and insert it back down at the top left corner of the same stitch. Pull the needle up again at the top right corner; then insert it back in at the lower left corner. Repeat this as many times as desired. It helps to sketch out a cross-stitch pattern on graph paper first. Try stitching flowers, geometric shapes, or letters.

breakfast

Breakfast is the most important meal of the day, right? It is sweet and savory, full of strong aromas like coffee, bacon, and maple syrup. Crochet your favorite dishes with unique scents to make a meal worth waking up for.

fried egg

Carb-free and high in protein, a fried egg that smells like butter or bacon starts your morning on the sunny side.

INSTRUCTIONS

Egg White Layer (Make 2):

Rnd 1: With A, make an adjustable ring, ch 1, work 6 sc in ring. Pull tail to close ring—6 sts. Do not join at end of each round until instructed. Place marker at beginning of round and move marker up as each round is completed.

Rnd 2: 2 sc in each st around—12 sts.

Rnd 3: *2 sc in next 3 sts, sc in next 3 sts; rep from * around—18 sts.

Rnd 4: Sc in next 2 sts, 2 hdc in next 3 sts, sc in next st, 2 hdc in next 3 sts, sc in next 9 sts—24 sts.

Rnd 5: Sc in next 3 sts, 2 hdc in next 3 sts, sc in next 3 sts, 2 hdc in next 3 sts, sc in next 12 sts; join with sl st in first st—30 sts.

- Fasten off, leaving a long tail for sewing.

- Repeat for a second egg white layer.

- Hold egg white layers together with wrong sides facing and sew together around the edges with the yarn tail. No stuffing is necessary.

Yolk:

Rnds 1–2: With B, repeat Rnds 1 and 2 of Egg White—12 sts.

Rnd 3: Sc in each st around; join with sl st in first st.

- Fasten off, leaving a long tail for sewing. With yarn needle, sew the yolk to the center of the egg white. Before sewing the last few stitches, insert the scent of your choice between the yolk and egg white. Weave in ends.

MATERIALS AND TOOLS

White worsted weight yarn (A) (4)

Yellow worsted weight yarn (B) (4)

Crochet hook: 3.25 mm (size D-3 U.S.)

Stitch marker

Yarn needle

Scent sachet: butter or bacon, page 6

STITCHES AND TECHNIQUES USED

Adjustable ring, page 11

Chain stitch (ch), page 9

Single crochet (sc), page 10

Half double crochet (hdc), page 13

Slip stitch (sl st), page 10

bacon

Crocheted bacon with a striped ripple pattern is easy to make. Make several strips to go with a crocheted Fried Egg (page 26) or make a sandwich with two slices of Toast (page 30) and as much Bacon as you want.

MATERIALS AND TOOLS

Maroon worsted weight yarn (A) **(4)**

Rust worsted weight yarn (B) **(4)**

Off-white worsted weight yarn (C) **(4)**

Crochet hook: 3.25 mm (size D-3 U.S.)

Scent sachet: bacon, page 6

Yarn needle

INSTRUCTIONS

Bacon Layer (Make 2):

Row 1 (RS): With A, ch 19, hdc in 3rd ch from hook and in each ch across—17 sts. Fasten off, leaving a short tail.

Row 2: With RS facing, join A with sc in first st, sc in next 2 sts, sk next st, sc in next 3 sts, 2 sc in next st, sc in next 3 sts, sk next st, sc in next 3 sts, 2 sc in next st, sc in last st—17 sts.

- Fasten off, leaving a short tail.

Row 3: With RS facing and B, rep Row 2.

Row 4: With RS facing and C, rep Row 2.

Row 5: With RS facing and B, rep Row 2.

- Fasten off, leaving a short tail. Weave in ends.

- Repeat for a second bacon layer.

- Hold the bacon layers together, wrong sides together, and sew around the edges with a strand of A. Before sewing the last few stitches, insert the scent of your choice between the layers.

STITCHES AND TECHNIQUES USED

Chain stitch (ch), page 9

Half double crochet (hdc), page 13

Single crochet (sc), page 10

Slip stitch (sl st), page 10

Changing color, page 20

toast

A warm and crunchy slice of toast can be a quick and simple breakfast, and the butter scent embedded in this crocheted version will smell like home.

INSTRUCTIONS

Crumb (Make 2):

Row 1: With A, ch 12, hdc in 3rd ch from hook and each ch across—10 sts.

Rows 2–4: Ch 2, turn, hdc in each st across.

Row 5: Ch 2, turn, 2 hdc in first st, hdc in next 8 sts, 2 hdc in last st—12 sts.

Row 6: Ch 2, turn, hdc2tog, hdc in 3 sts, sl st in next 2 sts, hdc in next 3 sts, hdc2tog—10 sts.

- Fasten off.

- Repeat for a second crumb.

Crust:

Rnd 1: Starting at the bottom right corner of one crumb and working ends of rows, join B with sc in first row, evenly space 8 sc across to top corner; working in top row, 2 sc in first st, evenly space 9 sc across to last st, 2 sc in last st; working in ends of rows of left edge, evenly space 9 sc across; working in opposite side of foundation chain, 2 sc in first ch, evenly space 9 sc across to last ch, 2 sc in last ch; join with sl st in first sc—42 sts.

- Fasten off, leaving a long tail. Hold pieces of toast with wrong sides together and seam with end tail and yarn needle. Before sewing the last few stitches, insert the scent of your choice. Weave in ends.

Finishing:

- If desired, use a bit of brown eye shadow or chalk to "toast" the bread. Apply sparingly with a cotton swab or your fingertip.

- For a jelly topping, use a permanent marker to color in an oblong shape on the surface of the toast. Allow to dry before handling.

MATERIALS AND TOOLS

Tan worsted weight yarn (A) **4**

Brown worsted weight yarn (B) **4**

Crochet hook: 3.25 mm (size D-3 U.S.)

Yarn needle

Scent sachet: butter, page 6

Brown eye shadow or chalk

Permanent marker for jelly (optional)

STITCHES AND TECHNIQUES USED

Chain stitch (ch), page 9

Single crochet (sc), page 10

Half double crochet (hdc), page 13

Half double crochet two together (hdc2tog), page 18

Changing color, page 20

bowl of cereal

I love cereal. Some nights I just want to line up boxes of cereal for dinner and call it a day, but I'm not sure my family would go along with it! Luckily, there's always crocheted cereal to the rescue. Crochet the bowl and milk, and use felt squares or colorful pompoms for cereal in your favorite flavor. Feel free to change the colors to whatever you like best.

INSTRUCTIONS

Bowl:

Rnd 1: With A, make an adjustable ring, ch 1, 6 sc in ring. Pull tail to close ring—6 sts. Do not join at end of each round until instructed. Place marker at beginning of round and move marker up as each round is completed.

Rnd 2: 2 sc in each st around—12 sts.

Rnd 3: *2 sc in next st, sc in next st; rep from * around—18 sts.

Rnd 4: Sl st in each st around.

Rnd 5: Working in Rnd 3, *2 sc in next st, sc in next 2 sts; rep from * around—24 sts.

Rnd 6: *2 sc in next st, sc in next 3 sts; rep from * around—30 sts.

Rnd 7: *2 sc in next st, sc in next 9 sts; rep from * around—33 sts.

Rnds 8–10: Sc in each st around; at end of Rnd 10, change color to B.

Rnd 11: Sl st in each st around; join with sl st in first st. Fasten off B.

Rnds 12–16: Join A with sl st in any st, ch 1, sc in each st around; at end of Rnd 16, join with sl st in first st—33 sts.

- Fasten off.

Rnd 17: Join C with sl st in any st; working in FLO, *sc2tog, sc in next 9 sts; rep from * around—30 sts.

Rnd 18: *Sc2tog, sc in next 3 sts; rep from * around—24 sts.

Rnd 19: *Sc2tog, sc in next 2 sts; rep from * around—18 sts.

- Place marker in last stitch made. Stuff the bowl with fiberfill up to the stripe in Rnd 11. Insert scent of your choice.

Rnd 20: *Sc2tog, sc in next st; rep from * around—12 sts.

Rnd 21: [Sc2tog] around; join with sl st in first st—6 sts.

MATERIALS AND TOOLS

Turquoise worsted weight yarn (A) **4**

Yellow worsted weight yarn (B) **4**

White worsted weight yarn (C) **4**

Crochet hook: 3.25 mm (size D-3 U.S.)

Stitch marker

Scent sachet: cinnamon, fruit, peanut butter, or chocolate, pages 6–7

Yarn needle

Polyester fiberfill

Light brown felt or multicolored or brown 5-mm pompoms for cereal

Craft glue

Dark brown or black permanent marker

- Fasten off, leaving a long tail. Weave tail through the last round and pull gently to close. Weave in ends.

Finishing:

- To create the bowl's rim, fold the top edges of the bowl inward so that the white "milk" is flush against the stuffing inside the cereal bowl. With a strand of A, straight-stitch around the top of the bowl to secure.

- For cinnamon-swirl cereal, cut as many ½-inch (1.2 cm) squares of felt as desired. With a permanent marker, draw swirls of "cinnamon" on each square. Glue to the surface of the milk.

- For fruity cereal, glue pompoms in a variety of colors to the surface of the milk.

- For peanut butter or chocolate cereal, glue only brown pompoms to the milk surface.

pancakes

For a sweet breakfast, nothing beats a stack of buttery pancakes with a good drizzle of maple syrup. Crochet as many as you want, stack them up, and top them with crocheted maple syrup and a pat of butter. The maple scent makes them all too real.

MATERIALS AND TOOLS

Light brown worsted weight yarn (A) **4**

Tan worsted weight yarn (B) **4**

Medium brown sport weight yarn (C) **2**

Yellow sport weight yarn (D) **2**

Crochet hooks: 2.75 mm (size C-2 U.S.) and 3.25 mm (size D-3 U.S.)

Stitch marker

Yarn needle

Scent sachet: maple, page 7

Craft glue (optional)

Dark blue plastic beads (optional)

STITCHES AND TECHNIQUES USED

Adjustable ring, page 11

Chain stitch (ch), page 9

Single crochet (sc), page 10

Slip stitch (sl st), page 10

Adjustable ring, page 11

Changing color, page 20

Back loops only (BLO), page 19

Half double crochet (hdc), page 13

INSTRUCTIONS

Pancake Layer (Make 2):

Rnd 1: With A and size D-3 hook, make an adjustable ring, ch 1, 6 sc in ring. Pull tail to close ring—6 sts. Do not join at end of each round until instructed. Place marker at beginning of round and move marker up as each round is completed.

Rnd 2: 2 sc in each st around—12 sts.

Rnd 3: *2 sc in next st, sc in next st; rep from * around—18 sts.

Rnd 4: *2 sc in next st, sc in next 2 sts; rep from * around—24 sts.

Rnd 5: *2 sc in next st, sc in next 3 sts; rep from * around—30 sts.

Rnd 6: *2 sc in next st, sc in next 4 sts; rep from * around; join with sl st in first st—36 sts.

- Fasten off, leaving a short tail.

- Repeat for a second pancake layer.

Edging rnd: Hold the layers with the wrong sides together. Working through both layers, join B with sl st in back loop of any st, sl st in BLO of each st around, inserting scent as work progresses—36 sts.

- Fasten off. Weave end tail through first st to join invisibly.

Syrup:

Rnd 1: With C and size C-2 hook, make an adjustable ring, ch 1, 6 sc in ring. Pull tail to close ring—6 sts.

Rnd 2: Ch 8, sc in 2nd ch from hook and in next 3 chs, sl st in last 3 chs, sc in first 2 sc of Rnd 1, ch 6, sc in 2nd ch from hook and in each ch across, sc in next sc, ch 11, hdc in 3rd ch from hook and in each ch across, sk next sc, sc in next sc, ch 5, sc in 2nd ch from hook and in each ch across, sc in last sc, ch 4, sc in 2nd ch from hook and in each ch across, sl st in last sc.

- Fasten off. Weave end tail through first st to join invisibly.

Butter:

Row 1: With D and size C-2 hook, ch 4, sc in 2nd ch from hook and in next 2 sts—3 sts.

Rows 2–3: Ch 1, turn, sc in each st—3 sts.

- Fasten off.

Finishing:

- Position the syrup on top of the pancake and sew or glue in place.

- Position the butter on top of the syrup and sew or glue in place. Weave in ends.

- For chocolate chip pancakes, add tiny brown felt circles to the tops of the pancakes with glue. Scent the pancakes with a chocolate scent sachet.

- For blueberry pancakes, sew or glue on dark blue pompoms or smooth plastic beads to the tops of the pancakes. Scent the pancakes with a blueberry scent sachet.

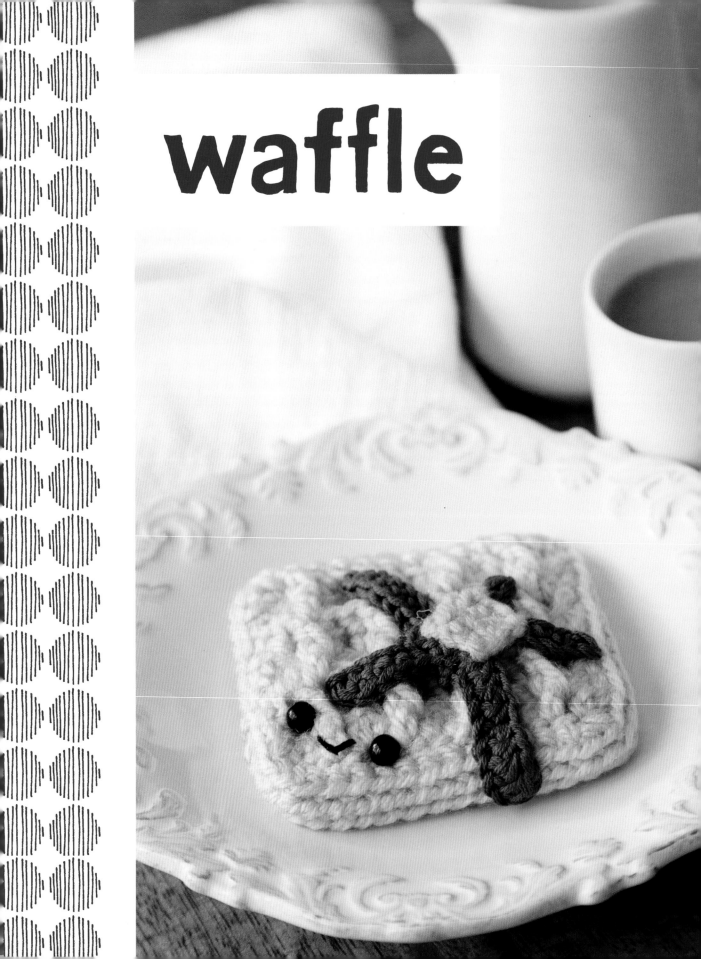

waffle

Crunchy on the outside and soft on the inside, waffles are another option for a sweet breakfast. A crocheted waffle stitch makes quick work of these square Belgian-style treats.

Skill Level:
EASY

INSTRUCTIONS

Waffle Layer (Make 2):

Row 1 (WS): With A and size D-3 hook, ch 14, dc in 3rd ch from hook and in next 11 chs—12 dc.

Row 2 (RS): Ch 2, turn, dc in first st, *FPdc around next st, dc in next 2 sts; rep from * twice, FPdc around next st, dc in last st—12 dc.

Row 3: Ch 2, turn, dc in first st, *dc in next st, FPdc around next 2 sts; rep from * twice, dc in last 2 sts—12 dc.

Rows 4–5: Rep Rows 2 and 3.

Row 6: Rep Row 2.

Row 7: Ch 1, *working in ends of rows, evenly space 11 sc across*; working in opposite side of foundation chain, 2 sc in first ch, evenly space 12 sc across to last ch, 2 sc in last ch; rep from * to *; working in top row, 2 sc in first st, evenly space 12 sc across to last st; join with sl st in first sc.

- Fasten off, leaving a long tail for sewing the waffle

layers together. With the wrong sides of the waffle layers held together, seam layers through BLO, inserting scent as the work progresses.

Syrup:

- Repeat Syrup pattern on page 37.

Butter:

- Repeat Butter pattern on page 37.

Finishing:

- Position the syrup on top of the waffle and sew or glue in place.

- Position the butter on top of the syrup and sew or glue in place. Weave in ends.

MATERIALS AND TOOLS

Light yellow worsted weight yarn (A) **4**

Medium brown sport weight yarn (B) brown **2**

Yellow sport weight yarn (C) **2**

Crochet hook: 2.75 mm (size C-2 U.S.) and 3.25 mm (size D-3 U.S.)

Scent sachet: maple, page 7

Yarn needle

Craft glue

STITCHES AND TECHNIQUES USED

Chain stitch (ch), page 9

Double crochet (dc), page 13

Front post double crochet (FPdc), page 16

Single crochet (sc), page 10

Slip stitch (sl st), page 10

Adjustable ring, page 11

Changing color, page 20

Back loops only (BLO), page 19

hot beverage mugs

Coffee really is the best part of waking up, am I right? Or maybe you like a cup of tea or hot cocoa to start your day? Whatever your pleasure, you can crochet a little mug in the color of your choice. Insert some coffee beans, a strong tea bag, or chocolate scent, and (pretend) drink to your heart's content.

Skill Level:
EASY

INSTRUCTIONS

Mug:

Rnd 1: With A, make an adjustable ring, ch 1, 6 sc in ring—6 sts. Do not join at end of each round until instructed. Place marker at beginning of round and move marker up as each round is completed.

Rnd 2: 2 sc in each st around—12 sts.

Rnd 3: *2 sc in first st, sc in next st; rep from * around—18 sts.

Rnd 4: *2 sc in next st, sc in next 2 sts; rep from * around—24 sts.

Rnd 5: *2 sc in next st, sc in next 3 sts; rep from * around—30 sts.

Rnd 6: Working in BLO, sc in each st around.

Rnds 7–15: Working in BLO, sc in each st around.

Rnds 16–17: Rep Rnds 6 and 7; change color to B at end of Rnd 17.

Rnd 18: Sl st in each st around.

Rnd 19: *Sc2tog, sc in next 3 sts; rep from * around—24 sts.

Rnd 20: *Sc2tog, sc in next 2 sts; rep from * around—18 sts.

- Place marker in last stitch made to hold your place. Stuff mug with fiberfill about two-thirds full and insert scent.

Rnd 21: *Sc2tog, sc in next st; rep from * around—12 sts.

Rnd 22: [Sc2tog] around; join with sl st in first st—6 sts.

- Fasten off, leaving a long tail. Weave the tail through the last round of the mug and pull gently to close. Fold the last two rounds inward to create the rim of the mug, keeping the top brown layer flat against the stuffing inside the mug. To secure, sew around the rim (Rnd 18) with embroidery floss in a matching color.

MATERIALS AND TOOLS

Worsted weight yarn in color of your choice (A) (4)

Light, medium, or dark brown worsted weight yarn (B) (4)

Crochet hook: 3.25 mm (size D-3 U.S.)

Stitch marker

Coffee, tea, or chocolate scent, pages 6–7

Yarn needle

Embroidery floss in color(s) of your choice

Embroidery needle

Polyester fiberfill

Felt in color(s) of your choice (optional)

White 5-mm pompoms (optional)

STITCHES AND TECHNIQUES USED

Adjustable ring, page 11

Chain stitch (ch), page 9

Single crochet (sc), page 10

Back loops only (BLO), page 19

Changing color, page 20

Single crochet two together (sc2tog), page 18

Slip stitch (sl st), page 10

Handle:

Rnd 1: With A, make an adjustable ring, ch 1, 6 sc in ring. Pull tail to close ring—6 sts. Do not join at end of each round until instructed. Place marker at beginning of round and move marker up as each round is completed.

Rnds 2–11: Sc in each st around; at end of last rnd, join with sl st in first sc.

- Fasten off, leaving a long tail. Flatten the handle and sew each end of the handle to the side of the mug using the yarn tail. Weave in ends.

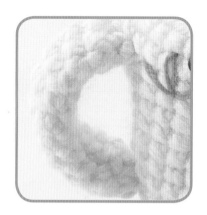

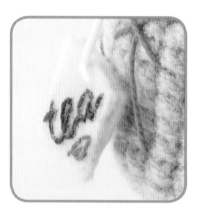

Finishing:

- Referring to the photo as a guide, decorate the outside of the mug with coordinating embroidery floss, or glue felt shapes where desired.

- To make a tea bag tag, cut a small square of felt, and with embroidery floss, sew *TEA* onto the felt with short back stitches. Hang the tag from the side of the mug with embroidery floss.

- To make marshmallows for a mug of cocoa, glue small white pompoms on the top brown layer.

juice carton and glass

Crochet this little carton and a glass of juice to go with your breakfast. Enhance both items with your favorite fruit scent for a fresh morning drink, and match yarn colors with your favorite flavor. A sturdy yarn works best for the carton so that the sides are stiff and retain their shape.

MATERIALS AND TOOLS

White worsted weight yarn (A) **(4)**

Worsted weight yarn in color of your juice (orange, yellow, purple, red, or any other fruit color) (B) **(4)**

Light gray worsted weight yarn (C) **(4)**

Crochet hook: 3.25 mm (size D-3 U.S.)

Scent sachet: orange, apple, grape, or any other fruit, pages 6–7

Yarn needle

Polyester fiberfill

Felt in color of fruit

Craft glue or embroidery floss and embroidery needle

STITCHES AND TECHNIQUES USED

Chain stitch (ch), page 9

Single crochet (sc), page 10

Back loops only (BLO), page 19

Adjustable ring, page 11

Single crochet two together (sc2tog), page 18

Slip stitch (sl st), page 10

Reverse single crochet (reverse sc), page 11

Changing color, page 20

INSTRUCTIONS

Carton:

BASE:

Row 1: With A, ch 11, sc in 2nd ch from hook and in each ch across—10 sts.

Rows 2–10: Ch 1, turn, sc in each st across.

- Fasten off, leaving a long tail.

RECTANGULAR PANEL:

Row 1: With A, ch 13, sc in 2nd ch from hook and in each ch across—12 sts.

Rows 2–10: Ch 1, turn, sc in each st across.

Row 11: Ch 1, turn, working in BLO, sc in each st across.

Rows 12–20: Ch 1, turn, working in both loops, sc in each st across.

Rows 21–40: Rep Rows 11–20 twice.

- Fasten off, leaving a long tail.

TOP PANEL:

Row 1: With A, ch 11, sc in 2nd ch from hook and in each ch across—10 sts.

Rows 2–20: Ch 1, turn, sc in each st across.

- Fasten off, leaving a long tail.

TRIANGULAR PANEL (MAKE 2):

Row 1: With A, ch 3, sc in 2nd ch from hook and in last ch—2 sts.

Row 2: Ch 1, turn, 2 sc in each st across—4 sts.

Rows 3–5: Ch 1, turn, 2 sc in first st, sc in each st across to last st, 2 sc in last st—10 sts at end of last row.

- Fasten off, leaving a long tail for sewing.

CARTON ASSEMBLY:

- To create the bottom of the carton, sew Row 1 of the rectangular panel to Row 40 with A. Sew the base to the bottom edge of the sewn rectangular panel.

- Fold the top panel in half. Weave tail to the beginning of Row 9 of the top panel and sew across this row. Sew the first and last rows of the top to the opposite edges of carton sides.

- Position one triangular panel in the opening between the top panel and the top edge of the rectangular panel. Sew in place. Insert fiberfill and scent; then sew the remaining triangular panel in place.

Glass:

Rnd 1: With B, make an adjustable ring, ch 1, 6 sc in ring. Pull tail to close ring—6 sts. Do not join at end of each round until instructed. Place marker at beginning of round and move marker up as each round is completed.

Rnd 2: 2 sc in each st around—12 sts.

Rnd 3: *2 sc in next st, sc in next st; rep from *

around—18 sts.

Rnd 4: *2 sc in next st, sc in next 2 sts; rep from * around—24 sts.

Rnd 5: Working in BLO, sc in each st around.

Rnds 6–12: Working in both loops, sc in each st around.

Rnd 13: Working in BLO, *sc2tog, sc in next 2 sts; rep from * around—18 sts.

Rnd 14: Working in both loops, *sc2tog, sc in next st; rep from * around—12 sts.

- Place marker in last stitch made to hold your place. Insert fiberfill and scent.

Rnd 15: [Sc2tog] around; join with sl st in first st—6 sts.

- Fasten off.

GLASS RIM:

Rnd 1: Join C with sl st in any unworked front loops of Rnd 13, ch 1, sc in each st around—24 sts. Do not join at end of each round until instructed. Place marker at beginning of round and move marker up as each round is completed.

Rnds 2 and 3: Sc in each st around.

Rnd 4: Ch 1, Reverse sc in each st around; join with sl st in first st.

- Fasten off. Weave in ends.

Finishing:

- Referring to the photo on page 43 as a guide, decorate the outside of carton with felt shapes of fruit. Cut the felt as desired. Glue or sew in place with embroidery thread and the embroidery needle. If desired, stitch details onto the felt with the embroidery floss and needle.

lunch

Do you love lunch? The perfect sandwich, accompanied by your favorite flavor of chips, a fresh piece of fruit, and a cold bottle of water is just the pick-me-up a lot of people need to keep the day moving. I really enjoy packing my kids' lunch boxes. I usually include a classic peanut butter and jelly or ham and cheese sandwich, but they also like the occasional left-over turkey leg or hot dog. I wonder how quickly they would notice if one of those items ended up being crocheted . . .

sandwich

Who can turn down this standard lunch box fare? From turkey and cheese to a simple peanut butter and jelly, a crocheted and scented sandwich makes lunchtime satisfying and complete. Change yarn colors for different types of bread and fillings.

Skill Level:
EASY

INSTRUCTIONS

Bread Slice (Make 2):

Row 1: With A, ch 12, hdc in 3rd ch from hook and in each ch across—10 sts.

Rows 2–4: Ch 2, turn, hdc in each st across.

Row 5: Ch 2, turn, 2 hdc in first st, hdc in next 8 sts, 2 hdc in last st—12 sts.

Row 6: Ch 2, turn, hdc2tog in first 2 sts, hdc in next 3 sts, sl st in next 2 sts, hdc in next 3 sts, hdc2tog—10 sts.

- Fasten off.

- Repeat for a second bread slice.

Crust and Fillings:

FOR FIRST SLICE OF BREAD:

Rnd 1: Starting at the bottom right corner of one slice of bread and working in ends of rows, join B with sc in first row, evenly space 9 sc across to top row; working in top row, 2 sc in first st, evenly space 10 sc across to last st, 2 sc in last st. Working in ends of rows of the left side of the bread slice, evenly space 10 sc across to first row; working in opposite side of foundation chain, 2 sc in first ch, evenly space 10 sc across to last ch, 2 sc in last ch; join with sl st in first sc—48 sts.

Rnd 2: Working in BLO, ch 1, sc in first 10 sts, [sc2tog, sc in next 10 sts] 3 times, sc2tog; change color to C for first sandwich filling; join with sl st in first sc—44 sts.

Rnd 3: Sl st in each st around; change color to D for second sandwich filling; do not join.

Rnd 4: Sc in each st around; join with sl st in first sc.

Rnd 5: Working in FLO, ch 1, *3 sc in next st, [sl st in next 3 sts, 3 sc in next st] twice, sl st in next 13 sts; rep from * around; join with sl st in first sc—56 sts.

- Fasten off.

Rnd 6: Working in unworked back loops, join E for a three-filling sandwich or C for a two-filling sandwich with sc in first st, sc in each remaining st around.

MATERIALS AND TOOLS

Off-white worsted weight yarn (A) **(4)**

Brown worsted weight yarn (B) **(4)**

Worsted weight yarn in filling color(s) of your choice (C), (D), and (E) **(4)**

Crochet hook: Size 3.25 mm (size D-3 U.S.)

Polyester fiberfill

Yarn needle

Scent sachet: mustard, peanut butter, or any scent of your choice, pages 6–7

STITCHES AND TECHNIQUES USED

Chain stitch (ch), page 9

Half double crochet (hdc), page 16

Half double crochet two together (hdc2tog), page 18

Slip stitch (sl st), page 10

Changing color, page 20

Back loops only (BLO), page 19

Note: If you would like to add additional fillings, change to desired color; working in both loops of each st, sc around.

Rnd 7: Sl st in each st around.

- Fasten off. Weave end tail through first st to join invisibly.

FOR SECOND SLICE OF BREAD:

Rnds 1–2: Rep Rnds 1 and 2 of Crust. Do not change to yarn C at the end of Rnd 2.

- Fasten off, leaving a long tail for sewing.

Assembly:

- Weave in ends. With wrong sides of Rnd 2 of the bread and the crusts and fillings held together, sew the pieces to each other, inserting the scent and fiberfill before sewing is completed.

Sandwich Menu

TYPE OF SANDWICH	FILLING COLORS (C, D, AND E)	SCENT
Turkey and cheese with lettuce	Pink, orange, and green	Mustard
BLT	Red and green	Bacon
Peanut butter and jelly	Tan and purple	Peanut butter
Grilled cheese	Orange and yellow	Cheese
Tuna Salad	Off-white and green	Dill
Reuben	Dark red and off-white	Rye bread

hot dog

It's hard to beat a grilled hot dog for a summer lunch. Some people like them plain, some like a squirt of mustard, and some like them piled with sauerkraut (yum—that's me). Be creative with your fixings. I've given you instructions for condiments and a fun way to make sauerkraut. Scent with dill, bacon-flavored salt, or mustard powder in a sachet.

MATERIALS AND TOOLS

Light brown worsted weight yarn (A) **4**

Off-white worsted weight yarn (B) **4**

Dark red worsted weight yarn (C) **4**

Gold or red worsted weight yarn (D) **4**

Crochet hook: Size 3.25 mm (size D-3 U.S.)

Stitch marker

Polyester fiberfill

Yarn needle

Straight pins

Scent sachet: dill, bacon, mustard, or any scent of your choice, pages 6–7

Thin off-white ribbon for sauerkraut (optional)

Green, orange, or yellow felt for toppings (optional)

STITCHES AND TECHNIQUES USED

Chain stitch (ch), page 9

Single crochet (sc), page 10

Slip stitch (sl st), page 10

Adjustable ring, page 11

Single crochet two together (sc2tog), page 18

INSTRUCTIONS

Bun:

OUTER TOP HALF:

Rnd 1: With A, ch 13, sc in 2nd ch from hook and in next 10 chs, 3 sc in last ch; working in opposite side of foundation chain, sk first ch, sc in next 11 chs, 3 sc in first sk ch—28 sts. Do not join at end of each round until instructed. Place marker at beginning of round and move marker up as each round is completed.

Rnd 2: *Sc in next 11 sts, 2 sc in next 3 sts; rep from * once—34 sts.

Rnd 3: Sc in next 13 sts, 2 sc in next 3 sts, sc in next 14 sts, 2 sc in next 3 sts, sc in next st—40 sts.

Rnd 4: Sc in next 15 sts, 2 sc in next 3 sts, sc in next 17 sts, 2 sc in next 3 sts, sc in next 2 sts—46 sts.

Rnds 5–8: Sc in each st around; at end of last rnd, join with sl st in first sc.

- Fasten off, leaving a long tail.

OUTER BOTTOM HALF:

Rnds 1–6: Rep Rnds 1–6 of Outer Top Half of Bun; at end of last rnd, join with sl st in first sc.

- Fasten off, leaving a long tail.

INNER HALF (MAKE 2):

Rnds 1–4: With B, rep Rnds 1–4 of Outer Top Half of Bun; at end of last rnd, join with sl st in first sc.

- Fasten off, leaving a long tail.

- Repeat for a second inner half.

Hot Dog:

Rnd 1: With C, make an adjustable ring, ch 1, 6 sc in ring. Pull tail to close ring— 6 sts. Do not join at end of each round until instructed. Place marker at beginning of round and move marker up as each round is completed.

Rnd 2: *2 sc in next st, sc in next st; rep from * around—9 sts.

Rnds 3–24: Sc in each st around.

- Place last stitch on stitch marker to hold your place, and stuff hot dog with fiberfill.

Rnd 25: *Sc2tog, sc in next st; rep from * around; join with sl st in first sc—6 sts.

- Fasten off, leaving a long tail. Use a yarn needle to weave the tail through the last round to close the hole.

Mustard or Ketchup:

- With D, ch 30. Fasten off, leaving a long tail.

Assembly:

- With wrong sides held together and stitches aligned, sew one Inner Half and the Outer Top Half of the bun together, inserting fiberfill and your chosen scent before stitching is complete. Repeat to sew sections of lower halves of bun together.

- With a strand of A, sew the long edges of the bun halves together.

- Pin mustard or ketchup across the hot dog in a wavy line. With end tail, sew in place.

- With end tail, sew hot dog into bun. Weave in ends.

Finishing:

- For sauerkraut, cut 18 strands of ribbon, each 4 inches (10.2 cm) long. Fold one strand in half to create a loop, insert your hook in a stitch on the inside of the bun close to the hot dog, pull up the loop of the ribbon, and pull the ribbon ends through loop to create a knot near the loop. Tighten to secure the ribbon. Repeat along both inner sides of the bun, using the remaining strands of ribbon. With sharp scissors, fray the ends of the ribbon.

- Try gluing tiny "diced" green felt for cute pickle relish, or skinny strips of orange and yellow felt for perfectly shredded cheese onto the hot dog.

turkey leg

If you're looking for a quick lunch at a theme park or country fair, nothing beats turkey legs. They tide everyone over until dinner. My kids love them. At Thanksgiving, they always fight over the turkey leg. Since I have three kids and, the last time I checked, most turkeys have two legs, someone misses out. Think they'll settle for a crocheted one next time?

INSTRUCTIONS

Rnd 1: With A, make an adjustable ring, ch 1, 6 sc in ring. Pull tail to close ring—6 sts. Do not join at end of each round until instructed. Place marker at beginning of round and move marker up as each round is completed.

Rnd 2: 2 sc in each st around—12 sts.

Rnd 3: *2 sc in next st, sc in next st; rep from * around—18 sts.

Rnd 4: *2 sc in next st, sc in next 2 sts; rep from * around—24 sts.

Rnds 5–7: Sc in each st around.

Rnd 8: *Sc2tog in next st, sc in next 6 sts; rep from * around—21 sts.

Rnd 9: Sc in each st around.

Rnd 10: *Sc2tog, sc in next 5 sts; rep from * around—18 sts.

Rnd 11: *Sc2tog, sc in next 4 sts; rep from * around—15 sts.

Rnd 12: *Sc2tog, sc in next 3 sts; rep from * around—12 sts.

Rnd 13: *Sc2tog, sc in next 4 sts; rep from * around—10 sts.

Rnd 14: *Sc2tog, sc in next 3 sts; rep from * around—8 sts.

Rnd 15: Sl st in each st around; then change color to B.

Rnds 16–17: Sc in each st around.

Rnd 18: 2 sc in each st around—16 sts.

Rnds 19–20: Sc in each st around.

Rnd 21: [Sc2tog] around—8 sts.

- Place last stitch on stitch marker to hold your place. Stuff with fiberfill and insert scent.

Rnd 22: *Sc2tog, sc in next 2 sts; rep from * around; join with sl st in first sc—6 sts.

- Fasten off, leaving a long tail. Weave tail through last round and pull gently to close.

MATERIALS AND TOOLS

Brown worsted weight yarn (A) [4]

Off-white worsted weight yarn (B) [4]

Crochet hook: 3.25 mm (size D-3 U.S.)

Stitch marker

Yarn needle

Polyester fiberfill

Scent sachet: poultry seasoning, page 7

STITCHES AND TECHNIQUES USED

Adjustable ring, page 11

Chain stitch (ch), page 9

Single crochet (sc), page 10

Single crochet two together (sc2tog), page 18

Slip stitch (sl st), page 10

Finishing:

- With the yarn needle, weave the end tail of B to the outside of the "bone" and pull tightly; sew over the end of bone and back inside, pulling tightly. Knot and weave yarn tail in. This creates the curved shape at the end of the bone. Weave in ends.

french fries

Why are simple sticks of deep-fried potatoes so good? And so bad for you? I guarantee you these crocheted fries are fat-free, so if you're still hungry after making these, just crochet more. They come in a little box, just like the one you'd get from a drive-thru window. They'll never get stale, and you'll never run out.

INSTRUCTIONS

Box:

Row 1: With A, ch 7, sc in 2nd ch from hook and in next 5 chs—6 sts.

Rows 2–3: Ch 1, turn, sc in each st across.

Rnd 4: Now working in rounds, ch 1, working in ends of rows, in opposite side of foundation chain, and across last row, evenly space 24 sc around—24 sts. Do not join at end of each round until instructed. Place marker at beginning of round and move marker up as each round is completed.

Rnd 5: Working in BLO, *sc2tog, sc in next 4 sts; rep from * around—20 sts.

Rnds 6–9: Sc in each st around.

Rnd 10: Hdc in next 4 sts, sl st in next 6 sts, hdc in next 2 sts, dc in next 8 sts; join with sl st in first hdc.

- Fasten off. Weave in ends.

French Fry (Make 5 or more):

Row 1: With B, ch 8, hdc in 3rd ch from hook and in each ch across—6 sts.

Row 2: Ch 2, turn, hdc in each st across.

- Repeat for four or more French fries.

- Fasten off, leaving a long yarn tail. Fold each French fry in half lengthwise and sew the first and last rows together with the yarn tail. Weave in ends. Insert fries into the box and sew to the bottom, if desired.

MATERIALS AND TOOLS

Red worsted weight yarn (A) (4)

Light yellow lightweight yarn (B) (3)

Crochet hook: 3.25 mm (size D-3 U.S.)

Stitch marker

Yarn needle

Scent sachet: French fry seasoning, page 6

STITCHES AND TECHNIQUES USED

Chain stitch (ch), page 9

Single crochet (sc), page 10

Back loops only (BLO), page 19

Half double crochet (hdc), page 13

Single crochet two together (sc2tog), page 18

Slip stitch (sl st), page 10

Double crochet (dc), page 13

pickle

The sourness of a crisp dill pickle spear makes it a perfect side for lots of different lunches. My local deli serves one with every order. My kids eat pickle popsicles made out of frozen pickle juice! Sweet or sour, pickles are fun to eat and fun to make. Scenting a crocheted pickle is as easy as filling a sachet with dill.

INSTRUCTIONS

Inside of Pickle (Make 2):

Row 1: With A, ch 14, 2 hdc in 3rd ch from hook, hdc next 10 chs, 3 hdc in last ch—15 hdc.

- Fasten off.

- Repeat for second pickle inside. Leave a long tail on this piece.

- Sew edges of Insides of Pickle together, working along the foundation chain edge.

Pickle Skin:

Row 1: With B, ch 3, sc in 2nd ch from hook and in last ch—2 sts.

Row 2: Ch 1, turn, 2 sc in each st—4 sts.

Row 3: Ch 1, turn, bobble [4 dc] in first st, sc in last 3 sts.

Row 4: Ch 1, turn, sc in each st across.

Row 5: Ch 1, turn, sc in first 2 sts, bobble [4 dc] in next st, sc in last st.

Row 6: Ch 1, turn, sc in each st across.

Row 7: Ch 1, turn, sc in first st, bobble [4 dc] in next st, sc in last 2 sts.

Row 8: Ch 1, turn, sc in each st across.

Row 9: Ch 1, turn, sc in first 3 sts, bobble [4 dc] in last st.

Rows 10–11: Ch 1, turn, sc in each st across.

Row 12: Ch 1, turn, [sc2tog] twice—2 sts.

Row 13: Ch 1, working in ends of rows, evenly space 28 sc around; join with sl st in first sc.

- Fasten off, leaving a long tail. Push all bobbles of the pickle skin out to the right side.

- Align the inside of the pickle with the pickle skin edge and sew together. Insert scent and stuffing before sewing is complete. Weave in ends.

MATERIALS AND TOOLS

Lime green worsted weight yarn (A) (4)

Medium green worsted weight yarn (B) (4)

Crochet hook: 3.25 mm (size D-3 U.S.)

Polyester fiberfill

Scent sachet: dill, page 6

Yarn needle

Craft glue

STITCHES AND TECHNIQUES USED

Chain stitch (ch), page 9

Half double crochet (hdc), page 13

Bobble stitch, page 15

Single crochet (sc), page 10

Single crochet two together (sc2tog), page 18

Slip stitch (sl st), page 10

apple

A crisp, red apple is one of the simple joys in life. Crocheting an apple can bring you joy too, especially when it is full of apple-scented goodness. If you prefer green or pink apples, just change the color of yarn A.

◇◇◇◇◇◇
Skill Level:
EASY
◇◇◇◇◇◇

INSTRUCTIONS

Fruit:

Rnd 1: Beginning at bottom of fruit, with A and D-3 hook, make an adjustable ring, ch 1, 6 sc in ring. Pull tail to close ring—6 sts. Do not join at end of each round until instructed. Place stitch marker at beginning of round and move marker up as each round is completed.

Rnd 2: 2 sc in each st around—12 sts.

Rnd 3: *2 sc in next st, sc in next st; rep from * around—18 sts.

Rnd 4: *2 sc in next st, sc in next 5 sts; rep from * around—21 sts.

Rnds 5–6: Sc in each st around.

Rnd 7: *2 sc in next st, sc in next 6 sts; rep from * around—24 sts.

Rnd 8: Sc in each st around.

Rnd 9: *2 sc in next st, sc in next 7 sts; rep from * around—27 sts.

Rnds 10–12: Sc in each st around.

Rnd 13: *2 sc in next st, sc in next 3 sts; rep from * around—30 sts.

Rnd 14: *Sc2tog, sc in next 3 sts; rep from * around—24 sts.

Rnd 15: [Sc2tog] around—12 sts.

- Place last stitch on stitch marker to hold your place. Stuff with fiberfill and insert scent.

Rnd 16: [Sc2tog] around; join with sl st in first sc—6 sts.

- Fasten off, leaving a long tail. Weave end tail through last round and pull tightly to close. Insert needle down through center hole and pull it out from center of Round 1. Pull tightly and knot.

Stem:

Row 1: With B and B-1 hook, ch 6, sc in 2nd ch from hook and in next 4 chs—5 sts.

- Fasten off, leaving a long tail. Sew the stem to the top of apple. Weave in ends.

MATERIALS AND TOOLS

Red worsted weight yarn (A) **4**

Brown fingering weight yarn (B) **4**

Crochet hooks: 2.25 mm (size B-1 U.S.) and 3.25 mm (size D-3 U.S.)

Stitch marker

Yarn needle

Polyester fiberfill

Scent sachet: apple, page 6

STITCHES AND TECHNIQUES USED

Adjustable ring, page 11

Chain stitch (ch), page 9

Single crochet (sc), page 10

Single crochet two together (sc2tog), page 18

Slip stitch (sl st), page 10

grapes

When I pack my kids' lunches, I like to give them a little bunch of grapes that they can pluck right off the stem. This crocheted bunch of grapes can be as full or as sparse as you'd like. Try making green or purple grapes with a grape scent.

INSTRUCTIONS

Grape
(Make at least 12):

Rnd 1: With A, make an adjustable ring, ch 1, 6 sc in ring. Pull tail to close ring—6 sts. Do not join at end of each round until instructed. Place marker at beginning of round and move marker up as each round is completed.

Rnd 2: *2 sc in next st, sc in next st; rep from * around—9 sts.

Rnds 3–4: Sc in each st around.

Rnd 5: *Sc2tog, sc in next st; rep from * around; join with sl st in first sc—6 sts.

- Fasten off, leaving a long tail.

- Repeat for additional grapes.

- Stuff each grape with a small amount of fiberfill, inserting scent in several, but not all, grapes. Weave end tail through last round and pull tightly. Knot the yarn in place and leave tail long for sewing to stem.

Stem:

Row 1: With B, ch 20, dc in 3rd ch from hook and in next 17 chs—18 sts.

- Fasten off, leaving a long tail. Fold stem in half lengthwise. With end tail, sew the long edges together.

Assembly:

- Starting at the bottom tip of the stem, sew grapes around the stem with their yarn tails, weaving in ends as you go. The grapes should be sewn on loosely so there is a little movement when they are handled. This makes them appear more realistic.

MATERIALS AND TOOLS

Dark purple or light green worsted weight yarn (A) **(4)**

Brown worsted weight yarn (B) **(4)**

Crochet hook: 3.25 mm (size D-3 U.S.)

Stitch marker

Polyester fiberfill

Yarn needle

Scent sachet: grape, page 6

STITCHES AND TECHNIQUES USED

Adjustable ring, page 11

Chain stitch (ch), page 9

Single crochet (sc), page 10

Single crochet two together (sc2tog), page 18

Slip stitch (sl st), page 10

bag of chips

This pattern is all that and a bag of chips. This interactive item belongs in any crocheted lunch. The bag features an opening in the top for tucking in a handful of little chips. Different flavors of chips are so easy to emulate using ranch seasoning, barbecue seasoning, or taco seasoning for my favorite, nacho cheese. Change the seasoning and bag color to make any kind you want.

Skill Level:
EASY

INSTRUCTIONS

Bag:

Rnd 1: With A and D-3 hook, ch 10, sc in 2nd ch from hook and in next 7 chs, 3 sc in last ch; working in opposite side of foundation chain, sk first ch, sc in next 8 chs—19 sts. Do not join at end of each round until instructed. Place marker at beginning of round and move marker up as each round is completed.

Rnds 2–7: Sc in each st around; at end of last rnd, join with sl st in first sc. Fasten off.

Rnd 8: Join B with sl st in first st, sl st in each remaining st around; change color to C.

Rnds 9–11: Sc in each st around.

Rnd 12: Working in BLO, sc2tog, sc in next 7 sts, sc2tog, sc in last 8 sts; join with sl st in first sc—17 sts.

- Fasten off, leaving a long tail. Stuff with fiberfill and scent. Flatten last round and with end tail, seam edges of last round together.

Rnd 13: Working in FLO of Rnd 11, join B with sl st in first st, sl st in each remaining st around; change color to A.

Rnd 14: Working in FLO of Rnd 11 again, sc in each st around.

Rnds 15–16: Sc in each st around; at end of last rnd, join with sl st in first sc.

MATERIALS AND TOOLS

Red worsted weight yarn (A) (4)

Orange worsted weight yarn (B) (4)

White worsted weight yarn (C) (4)

Yellow lightweight yarn (D) (3)

Crochet hooks: 2.25 mm (size B-1 U.S.) and 3.25 mm (size D-3 U.S.)

Stitch marker

Polyester fiberfill

Black embroidery floss

Embroidery needle

Yarn needle

Scent sachet: taco seasoning, ranch seasoning, barbecue seasoning, or any scent of your choice, pages 6–7

STITCHES AND TECHNIQUES USED

Chain stitch (ch), page 9

Single crochet (sc), page 10

Back loops only (BLO), page 19

Front loops only (FLO), page 19

Slip stitch (sl st), page 10

Treble crochet (tr), page 14

- Fasten off, leaving a long yarn tail. Flatten the bag, holding the edges of the last round together. With end yarn tail, sew the top edges together, leaving 1 inch (2.5 cm) open. Weave in ends.

Chips (Make 3 or more):

Row 1: With D and B-1 hook, ch 5, sc in 2nd ch from hook, hdc in next ch, dc in next ch, tr in last ch—4 sts.

- Repeat for additional chips.

- Fasten off. Weave in ends.

Finishing:

- With black embroidery floss, embroider *CHIPS* or any desired phrase with straight stitches across the white section of the bag. Use the crocheted stitches and rows as a grid to make even lettering. Place chips inside the top of the bag.

water bottle

A crocheted water bottle makes sense. I wouldn't put real water in it, of course, because of the holes. However, in a little crocheted lunch, it completes the picture, doesn't it? And you don't have to add scent if you're making plain old water. If you'd like to add a sturdy base to your water bottle, cut a piece of cardboard or plastic canvas to size and insert it before stuffing. Prefer something fruity? Cola? Change the yarns colors and add the matching scent to easily make your favorite drink.

MATERIALS AND TOOLS

Pale blue worsted weight yarn (A) **4**

White worsted weight yarn (B) **4**

Light gray worsted weight yarn (C) **4**

Crochet hook: 3.25 mm (size D-3 U.S.)

Stitch marker

Polyester fiberfill

Yarn needle

Embroidery needle

Black (or color of your choice) embroidery floss

Plastic canvas or sturdy cardboard cut to fit bottom of bottle (optional)

STITCHES AND TECHNIQUES USED

Adjustable ring, page 11

Chain stitch (ch), page 9

Single crochet (sc), page 10

Back loops only (BLO), page 19

Front loops only (FLO), page 19

Single crochet two together (sc2tog), page 18

Slip stitch (sl st), page 10

INSTRUCTIONS

Rnd 1: Starting at bottom of bottle, with A, make an adjustable ring, ch 1, 6 sc in ring. Pull tail to close ring—6 sts. Do not join at end of each round until instructed. Place marker at beginning of round and move marker up as each round is completed.

Rnd 2: 2 sc in each st around—12 sts.

Rnd 3: *2 sc in next st, sc in next st; rep from * around—18 sts.

Rnd 4: *2 sc in next st, sc in next 2 sts; rep from * around—24 sts.

Rnd 5: Working in BLO, sc in each st around—24 sts.

Rnd 6: Working in both loops of each st, sc in each st around.

Rnd 7: Working in BLO, 2 sc in each st around—48 sts.

Rnd 8: Working in FLO, [sc2tog] around—24 sts.

Rnds 9–12: Rep Rnds 7 and 8 twice; at end of last rnd, change color to B.

Rnd 13: Rep Rnd 5.

Rnds 14–17: Sc in each st around; at end of last rnd, change color to A.

Rnds 18–24: Rep Rnds 7–13.

Rnd 25: *Sc2tog, sc in next 6 sts; rep from * around; change color to C—21 sts.

- Place last stitch on stitch marker to hold your place. If desired, insert a round piece of cardboard or plastic canvas cut to size in the bottom of your bottle to help the bottle stand by itself. Stuff bottle with fiberfill, adding more as work progresses.

Rnd 26: *Sc2tog, sc in next 5 sts; rep from * around—18 sts.

Rnd 27: *Sc2tog, sc in next st; rep from * around— 12 sts.

Rnd 28: *Sc2tog, sc in next 2 sts; rep from * around— 9 sts.

Rnd 29: Sc in each st around; change color to B.

Rnd 30: Sl st in each st around.

Rnds 31–32: Sc in each st around—9 sts.

Rnd 33: Working in BLO, *sc2tog, sc in next st; rep from * around; join with sl st in first sc—6 sts.

- Fasten off. Weave end tail through last round and pull tightly to close.

Finishing:

- With embroidery floss, embroider *WATER* with straight stitches across the white label section of the bottle. Use the crocheted stitches and rows as a grid for letter placement and sizing.

dinner

When I cook dinner, I don't necessarily stick to the same basic meals every week, and I like to try new recipes from lots of different cuisines. The same can be said for my crocheting style! What can I say? Variety is the spice of life. Here, you'll find a variety of plush meals and sides to make a playful and fun scented meal you can serve your family. There will be plenty to go around, and you'll always have leftovers.

tacos

Crunchy or soft, tacos are a staple food in Texas, where I live. We eat them for breakfast, lunch, and dinner, so it's only natural I'd crochet a couple. By changing the colors of the tortilla and fillings, you can make flour or corn tortillas with beef, chicken, or beans. Add crocheted lettuce and cheese, if you like.

Skill Level:
EASY

INSTRUCTIONS

Tortilla:

Rnd 1: With A, make an adjustable ring, ch 1, 6 sc in ring. Pull tail to close ring—6 sts. Do not join at end of each round until instructed. Place marker at beginning of round and move marker up as each round is completed.

Rnd 2: 2 sc in each st around—12 sts.

Rnd 3: *2 sc in next st, sc in next st; rep from * around—18 sts.

Rnd 4: *Sc in next st, 2 sc in next st, sc in next st; rep from * around—24 sts.

Rnd 5: *Sc in next 2 sts, 2 sc in next st, sc in next st; rep from * around—30 sts.

Rnd 6: *Sc in next st, 2 sc in next st, sc in next 3 sts; rep from * around—36 sts.

Rnd 7: *Sc in next 4 sts, 2 sc in next st, sc in next st; rep from * around—42 sts.

Rnd 8: *Sc in next 2 sts, 2 sc in next st, sc in next 4 sts; rep from * around—48 sts.

Rnd 9: *Sc in next 7 sts, 2 sc in next st; rep from * around; join with sl st in first sc—54 sts.

- Fasten off.

Meat:

Row 1 (RS): With B, ch 7, bobble [4 dc] in 2nd ch from hook, sc in next 2 chs, bobble [4 dc] in next ch, sc in last 2 chs—6 sts.

Row 2: Ch 1, turn, sc in each st across.

Row 3: Ch 1, turn, sc in first 2 sts, bobble [4 dc] in next st, sc in next 2 sts, bobble [4 dc] in last st.

MATERIALS AND TOOLS

Off-white or light yellow worsted weight yarn (A) **4**

Brown worsted weight yarn (B) **4**

Light orange worsted weight yarn (C) **4**

Light green worsted weight yarn (D) **4**

Crochet hook: 3.25 mm (size D-3 U.S.)

Stitch marker

Yarn needle

Scent sachet: taco seasoning, page 7

STITCHES AND TECHNIQUES USED

Adjustable ring, page 11

Chain stitch (ch), page 9

Single crochet stitch (sc), page 10

Slip stitch (sl st), page 10

Bobble stitch, page 15

Double crochet (dc), page 13

Row 4: Ch 1, turn, sc in each st across.

Row 5: Ch 1, turn, bobble [4 dc] in first st, sc in next 2 sts, bobble [4 dc] in next st, sc in next 2 sts.

Rows 6–13: Rep Rows 2–5 twice.

- Fasten off.

Cheese:

- With an 18-inch (46 cm) long strand of C, embroider short straight stitches all over the top of the meat as desired. Weave in ends.

Lettuce:

Row 1: With D, ch 11, (3 dc, sc) in 2nd ch from hook and in next 8 chs, 6 dc in last ch; working in opposite side of foundation chain, (sc, 3 dc) in each ch across—78 sts.

- Fasten off, leaving a long tail.

Assembly:

- For a crunchy taco, fold the meat lengthwise, place in the center of the tortilla, and sew in place with a strand of A. Fold the lettuce in half lengthwise, and with end tail, sew to meat. Weave in ends.

- For a soft taco, the tortilla will be wrapped around the meat. With a strand of A, sew the edges of the meat to the tortilla; then fold the sides of the tortilla closed around the meat, overlapping the edges. Weave in ends.

avocado

Avocados are a staple that we eat with all of our Mexican meals, and they are especially great with tacos. This crocheted avocado can be scented with guacamole seasoning.

INSTRUCTIONS

Skin (Make 2):

Rnd 1: With A, ch 7, sc in 2nd ch from hook and in next 4 chs, 6 hdc in last ch; working in opposite side of foundation chain, sc in next 5 chs—16 sts. Do not join at end of each round until instructed. Place stitch marker at beginning of round and move marker up as each round is completed.

Rnd 2: Sc in next 5 sts, *2 hdc in next st, hdc in next st; rep from * twice, sc in next 5 sts—19 sts.

Rnd 3: 2 sc in next st, sc in next 8 sts, 2 sc in next st, sc in next 9 sts—21 sts.

Rnd 4: *2 sc in next st, sc in next 6 sts; rep from * around—24 sts.

Rnd 5: Sc in each st around; join with sl st in first sc.

- Fasten off.

- Repeat for a second skin.

Pulp (Make 2):

Rnd 1: With B, make an adjustable ring, ch 1, 6 sc in ring. Pull tail to close ring— 6 sts. Do not join at end of each round until instructed. Place stitch marker at beginning of round and move marker up as each round is completed.

Rnd 2: *2 sc in next st, sc in next st; rep from * around—9 sts.

Rnd 3: *2 sc in next st, sc in next 2 sts; rep from * around—12 sts.

Rnd 4: Working in BLO, *2 sc in next st, sc in next st; rep from * around—18 sts.

Rnd 5: Ch 6, dc in 4th ch from hook, dc in next ch, tr in next ch, sk next 3 sts of Rnd 4, sl st in next st; leave remaining sts unworked.

- Fasten off, leaving a long tail. With the end tail, sew the space between treble crochet of Rnd 5 and the unworked stitches of Rnd 4 closed. Weave in ends.

- Repeat for a second pulp.

Pit:

Rnd 1: With C, make an adjustable ring, ch 1, 6 sc in ring. Pull tail to close ring— 6 sts.

- Do not join at end of each round until instructed. Place stitch marker at beginning of round and move marker up as each round is completed.

Rnd 2: 2 sc in each st around—12 sts.

Rnd 3: Sc in each st around.

Rnd 4: [Sc2tog] around, stuffing as you work final stitches; join with sl st in first sc—6 sts.

- Fasten off, leaving a long tail. Gently pull the tail through the last round to close the ring. Weave in ends.

Assembly:

- Align the pulp with the skin and sew in place with a strand of yarn B, adding the scent and polyester fiberfill before completing the stitching.

- Sew the pit in place on one avocado half with C. On the other avocado half, push Rnds 1–3 of the pulp down into the avocado.

spaghetti with meatballs & sauce

One of my favorite Italian dishes, spaghetti and meatballs, is one meal I keep on rotation. It's a crowd-pleaser and quick to make, just like this crocheted version! Italian seasoning stuffed inside the little meatballs makes this spaghetti dinner realistically fragrant.

INSTRUCTIONS

Spaghetti:

Row 1 (RS): With A, ch 500 or make a crocheted chain approximately 8½ feet (2.6 m) long.

- Fasten off. Weave in yarn ends before assembling.

Sauce:

Rnd 1: With B, make an adjustable ring, ch 1, 6 sc in ring. Pull tail to close ring—6 sts. Do not join at end of each round until instructed. Place stitch marker at beginning of round and move marker up as each round is completed.

Rnd 2: 2 sc in each st around—12 sts.

Rnd 3: *2 sc in next st, sc in next st; rep from * around—18 sts.

Rnd 4: *Sc in next st, 2 sc in next st, sc in next st; rep from * around—24 sts.

Rnd 5: *Hdc in next st, dc in next 2 sts, hdc in next st, sc in next 4 sts; rep from * around—24 sts.

Rnd 6: *Sc in next st, 3 dc in next st, sc in next st; rep from * around; join with sl st in first sc—40 sts.

- Fasten off, leaving a long tail.

Meatballs (Make 3 or more):

Rnd 1: With C, make an adjustable ring, ch 1, 6 sc in ring. Pull tail to close ring—6 sts. Do not join at end of each round until instructed. Place stitch marker at beginning of round and move marker up as each round is completed.

MATERIALS AND TOOLS

Off-white worsted weight yarn (A) 4

Burgundy worsted weight yarn (B) 4

Brown worsted weight yarn (C) 4

Crochet hook: 3.25 mm (size D-3 U.S.)

Stitch marker

Yarn needle

Polyester fiberfill

Scent sachet: Italian seasoning, page 7

STITCHES AND TECHNIQUES USED

Chain stitch (ch), page 9

Adjustable ring, page 11

Single crochet (sc), page 10

Half double crochet (hdc), page 13

Double crochet (dc), page 13

Slip stitch (sl st), page 10

Single crochet two together (sc2tog), page 18

Rnd 2: *2 sc in next st, sc in next 3 sts; rep from * around—15 sts.

Rnd 3: Sc in each st around.

Rnd 4: *Sc2tog, sc in next 3 sts; rep from * around— 12 sts.

- Place last stitch on stitch marker to prevent unraveling. Stuff with fiberfill and insert scent.

Rnd 5: [Sc2tog] around; join with sl st in first sc—6 sts.

- Fasten off, leaving a long tail. Using the yarn needle and yarn tail, sew the last round closed. Weave in ends.

- Repeat for additional meatballs.

Assembly:

- Sew each meatball to the sauce with matching yarn.

- Arrange the long spaghetti strand in a pile. Place the sauce on top of the pile. With the remaining tail of the sauce, sew through all the layers of the spaghetti all around, securing the sauce to the pile. Weave in yarn ends.

buffalo wings

Skill Level:
EASY

MATERIALS AND TOOLS

Rust worsted weight yarn (A) 〔4〕

Crochet hook: 3.25 mm (size D-3 U.S.)

Stitch marker

Yarn needle

Polyester fiberfill

Scent sachet: buffalo wing seasoning, page 6

STITCHES AND TECHNIQUES USED

Adjustable ring, page 11

Chain stitch (ch), page 9

Single crochet (sc), page 10

Single crochet two together (sc2tog), page 18

Slip stitch (sl st), page 10

Hot and spicy buffalo chicken wings are a favorite at my house. This crochet pattern has the two standard wing shapes, drumettes and flats, so you can have a full serving for your next amigurumi dinner. Stuff each one with a little buffalo wing seasoning mix for a realistic touch.

INSTRUCTIONS

Drumettes:

Rnd 1: With A, make an adjustable ring, ch 1, 6 sc in ring. Pull tail to close ring—6 sts. Do not join at end of each round until instructed. Place stitch marker at beginning of round and move marker up as each round is completed.

Rnd 2: 2 sc in each st around—12 sts.

Rnds 3–5: Sc in each st around.

Rnds 6–11: Sc2tog, sc in each remaining st around—6 sts after completing Rnd 11.

- Place last stitch on stitch marker to prevent unraveling. Stuff with fiberfill and insert desired scent.

Rnd 12: *2 sc in next st, sc in next st; rep from * around—9 sts.

Rnd 13: Sc in each st around.

Rnd 14: *Sc2tog, sc in next st; rep from * around; join with sl st in first sc—6 sts.

- Fasten off, leaving a long tail. With yarn needle, weave the end tail through the last round of each piece and pull gently to close. Weave in ends.

Flats:

Rnd 1: With A, make an adjustable ring, ch 1, 6 sc in ring. Pull tail to close ring—6 sts. Do not join at end of each round until instructed. Place stitch marker at beginning of round and move marker up as each round is completed.

Rnd 2: *2 sc in next st, sc in next 2 sts; rep from * around—8 sts.

Rnd 3: 2 sc in next st, sc in each st around—9 sts.

Rnd 4: Sc in each st around.

Rnd 5: 2 sc in next st, sc in each st around—10 sts.

Rnds 6–7: Sc in each st around.

Rnd 8: *2 sc in next st, sc in next 4 sts; rep from * around—12 sts.

Rnds 9–10: Sc in each st around.

Rnd 11: *Sc2tog, sc in next 2 sts; rep from * around—9 sts.

Rnd 12: Sc in each st around.

- Place last stitch on stitch marker to prevent unraveling. Stuff with fiberfill and insert scent.

Rnd 13: *Sc2tog, sc in next st; rep from * around; join with sl st in first sc—6 sts.

- Fasten off, leaving a long tail for sewing. With yarn needle, weave the end tail through the last round of each piece and pull gently to close. Weave in ends.

pizza slices

Nothing hits the spot like some pizza on a Friday night. From a sophisticated slice of Margherita pizza to simple pepperoni, this crocheted pizza pattern is fun and works up quickly. Hide your scent of choice between the dough and the sauce; then pile on the toppings. Crochet mozzarella, basil, or pepperoni, and cut shapes from colored felt for anything else, from mushrooms and peppers to my favorite, pineapple. To create the perfectly toasted crust, use brown and dark gray eye shadows to lightly color the edges.

INSTRUCTIONS

Dough:

Row 1 (RS): With A and leaving a 12-inch (30.5 cm) tail, ch 21, sc in 2nd ch from hook and in next 19 chs—20 sts.

Row 2: Ch 1, turn, sc in each st across.

Row 3 and all odd-numbered rows: Ch 1, turn, sc in each st across.

Row 4: Ch 2, turn, hdc2tog, hdc in next 16 sts, hdc2tog—18 sts.

Row 6: Ch 2, turn, hdc2tog, hdc in next 14 sts, hdc2tog—16 sts.

Row 8: Ch 2, turn, hdc2tog, hdc in next 12 sts, hdc2tog—14 sts.

Row 10: Ch 2, turn, hdc2tog, hdc in next 10 sts, hdc2tog—12 sts.

Row 12: Ch 2, turn, hdc2tog, hdc in next 8 sts, hdc2tog—10 sts.

Row 14: Ch 2, turn, hdc2tog, hdc in next 6 sts, hdc2tog—8 sts.

Row 16: Ch 2, turn, hdc2tog, hdc in next 4 sts, hdc2tog—6 sts.

Row 18: Ch 2, turn, hdc2tog, hdc in next 2 sts, hdc2tog—4 sts.

Row 20: Ch 2, turn, [hdc2tog] twice—2 sts.

Row 21: Ch 1, turn, sc in each st across.

- Fasten off. To form the crust, fold the first couple of rows down and sew in place with yarn tail. Weave in ends.

Skill Level:
EASY

MATERIALS AND TOOLS

Beige worsted weight yarn (A) **4**

Red worsted weight yarn (B) **4**

White worsted weight yarn (C) **4**

Green worsted weight yarn (D) **4**

Dark red worsted weight yarn (E) **4**

Crochet hook: 3.25 mm (size D-3 U.S.)

Stitch marker

Yarn needle

Polyester fiberfill

Scent sachet: Italian seasoning, page 7

Brown and dark gray eye shadow or chalk (optional)

STITCHES AND TECHNIQUES USED

Chain stitch (ch), page 9

Half double crochet two together (hdc2tog), page 18

Half double crochet (hdc), page 13

Single crochet (sc), page 10

Slip stitch (sl st), page 10

Adjustable ring, page 11

Sauce:

Row 1 (RS): With B, ch 18, hdc in 3rd ch from hook and in each ch across—16 sts.

Row 2: Ch 1, turn, sc in each st across.

Row 3: Ch 2, turn, hdc2tog, hdc in next 12 sts, hdc2tog —14 sts.

Rows 4–16: Rep Rows 9–21 of Crust with B.

- Fasten off, leaving a long tail for sewing. Place the sauce on the crust. With yarn tail, sew completely around the edge, adding your chosen scent and some fiberfill before finishing. Weave in ends.

Pepperoni Pizza:

Classic pepperoni pizza is a crowd-pleaser. Start with sauce and a full layer of cheese, then top it with whole and half slices of pepperoni.

CHEESE:

Row 1 (RS): With C, ch 17, sc in 2nd ch from hook and in each ch across—16 sts.

Row 2: Ch 2, turn, hdc2tog, hdc in next 12 sts, hdc2tog —14 sts.

Rows 3–15: Repeat Rows 9–21 of Crust.

- Fasten off, leaving a long tail.

Top Edge Row: With RS of Row 1 facing, join C with sc in first st, *hdc in next 2 sts, sc in next st, sl st in next 2 sts, sc in next st; repeat from * once, hdc in next 2 sts, sc in last st.

- Fasten off, leaving a long tail for sewing.

PEPPERONI ROUND (MAKE 3 OR MORE):

Rnd 1: With E, make an adjustable ring, ch 1, 6 sc in ring. Pull tail to close ring— 6 sts. Do not join.

Rnd 2: 2 sc in each st around; join with sl st in first sc— 12 sts.

- Fasten off, leaving a long tail for sewing.

- Repeat for additional pepperoni pieces.

PEPPERONI HALF ROUNDS (MAKE 3 OR MORE):

Rnd 1: With E, make an adjustable ring, ch 1, 3 sc in ring. Pull tail to close ring— 3 sts. Do not join.

Rnd 2: Ch 1, turn, 2 sc in each st across—6 sts.

- Fasten off, leaving a long tail for sewing.

- Repeat for additional pepperoni halves.

Margherita Pizza:

If you'd like a traditional Neapolitan style pizza, you'll add sliced fresh mozzarella cheese to the sauce layer. Crocheted basil adds even more color and flavor.

MOZZARELLA CHEESE (MAKE 2 OR MORE):

Rnd 1: With C, ch 4, sc in 2nd ch from hook and in next ch, 5 sc in last ch; working in opposite side of foundation chain, sc in next 2 chs, 5 sc in beginning ch—14 sts. Do not join at end of each round until instructed. Place stitch marker at beginning of round and move marker up as each round is completed.

Rnd 2: Sc in next 4 sts, 2 sc in next 2 sts, sc in next 5 sts, 2 sc in next 2 sts—17 sts.

Rnd 3: Sc in next 6 sts, sl st in next st; leave remaining sts unworked—7 sts.

- Fasten off, leaving a long tail for sewing.

BASIL:

Row 1: With yarn D, ch 6, sc in 2nd ch from hook and in next ch, hdc in next 2 chs, 7 dc in last ch; working in opposite side of foundation chain, hdc in next 2 chs, sc in next ch, sl st in last ch—15 sts.

- Fasten off, leaving a long tail for sewing.

Assembly:

- For the Pepperoni Pizza, place the cheese on the sauce and sew it in place around the edge with yarn tails. Weave in ends. Sew the whole pepperoni slices on the inside area of the pizza. Sew the pepperoni halves along the edges. Weave in ends.

- For the Margherita Pizza, sew the mozarella cheese and basil where desired to the sauce. Weave in ends.

Finishing:

- If desired, apply eye shadow or colored chalk with a cotton swab or your fingertip to add coloring to the crust edges. Repeat for the edges of the cheese.

lemon-baked fish

I don't normally like to eat food that has a head, but how cute is this crocheted baked fish? This one has lemon slices on top and little *x*'s for eyes. Scent with lemon pepper seasoning or lemon extract for a fun twist.

INSTRUCTIONS

Fish Body and Head:

Rnd 1: Starting at head, with A, make an adjustable ring, ch 1, 6 sc in ring. Pull tail to close ring—6 sts. Do not join at end of each round until instructed. Place marker at beginning of round and move marker up as each round is completed.

Rnd 2: *2 sc in next st, sc in next st; rep from * around—9 sts.

Rnd 3: *2 sc in next st, sc in next 2 sts; rep from * around—12 sts.

Rnd 4: *2 sc in next st, sc in next 3 sts; rep from * around—15 sts.

Rnd 5: *2 sc in next st, sc in next 4 sts; rep from * around—18 sts.

Rnd 6: *2 sc in next st, sc in next 5 sts; rep from * around—21 sts.

- Hold a strand of black embroidery floss together with A for the rest of the body.

Rnds 7–18: Sc in each st around.

Rnd 19: *Sc2tog, sc in next 5 sts; rep from * around—18 sts.

Rnd 20: *Sc2tog, sc in next 4 sts; rep from * around—15 sts.

Rnd 21: *Sc2tog, sc in next 3 sts; rep from * around—12 sts.

Rnd 22: Sc in each st around; join with sl st in first sc.

- Fasten off, leaving a long yarn tail. Stuff fish with fiberfill and insert scent. Flatten the last round and sew through both thicknesses of stitches with yarn tail to close. Weave in ends.

Fish Tail:

Row 1 (RS): With A, ch 7, sc in 2nd ch from hook and in each ch across—6 sts.

Row 2: Ch 1, turn, working in BLO, sc in first 2 sts, hdc in next 2 sts, dc in last 2 sts.

MATERIALS AND TOOLS

Silver worsted weight yarn (A) (4)

Light yellow worsted weight yarn (B) (4)

Medium yellow worsted weight yarn (C) (4)

Crochet hook: 3.25 mm (size D-3 U.S.)

Stitch marker

Scent sachet: lemon pepper or lemon, page 7

Polyester fiberfill

Yarn needle

Embroidery needle

Black embroidery floss

White embroidery floss

STITCHES AND TECHNIQUES USED

Adjustable ring, page 11

Chain stitch (ch), page 9

Single crochet (sc), page 10

Single crochet two together (sc2tog), page 18

Slip stitch (sl st), page 10

Back loops only (BLO), page 19

Front loops only (FLO), page 19

Treble crochet (tr), page 14

Row 3: Ch 3, turn, working in FLO, dc in first 2 sts, hdc in next 2 sts, sc in last 2 sts.

Rows 4–5: Rep Rows 2 and 3.

Row 6: Rep Row 2.

- Fasten off, leaving a long yarn tail. Sew the Fish Tail to end of the Fish Body. Weave in ends.

Fin (Make 2):

Row 1: With A, ch 5, sc in 2nd ch from hook, hdc in next ch, dc in next ch, tr in last ch—4 sts.

- Fasten off, leaving a long yarn tail.

- Repeat for a second fin.

- Sew the fins to the top and bottom of the fish body. Weave in ends.

Lemon Slice (Make 3):

Rnd 1: With B, make an adjustable ring, ch 1, 6 sc in ring. Pull tail to close ring— 6 sts. Do not join at end of each round until instructed. Place stitch marker at beginning of round and move marker up as each round is completed.

Rnd 2: 2 sc in each st around; change color to C in last st—12 sts.

Rnd 3: Sl st in each st around.

- Fasten off, leaving a long yarn tail. Weave end tail through first st to join invisibly. Do not trim.

- With white embroidery floss and an embroidery needle, embroider straight stitches on each lemon slice to outline the segments in the center.

- Repeat for additional lemon slices.

Finishing:

- Place the lemon slices on the body and sew in place. Weave in ends.

- Thread an embroidery needle with black embroidery floss. Stitch an *x* on each side of the head for the eyes. Stitch a diagonal line for the fish's mouth.

baked potato

For a quick dinner, a baked potato can be a satisfying choice. I like it with just butter, but you can add any toppings you'd like. Make shredded cheese by straight-stitching orange yarn over the top of the potato, or add bacon bits by gluing dark red felt pieces in place. Scent with butter-flavored seasoning for a realistic touch.

MATERIALS AND TOOLS

Brown worsted weight yarn (A) **4**

Off-white worsted weight yarn (B) **4**

Yellow lightweight yarn (C) **2**

Orange yarn for cheese, any weight (optional)

Crochet hooks: 2.75 mm (size C-2 U.S.) and 3.25 mm (size D-3 U.S.)

Stitch marker

Yarn needle

Long pins

Polyester fiberfill

Scent sachet: butter, page 6

Dark red felt (optional)

Dark green felt (optional)

Craft glue (optional)

STITCHES AND TECHNIQUES USED

Adjustable ring, page 11

Chain stitch (ch), page 9

Single crochet (sc), page 10

Single crochet two together (sc2tog), page 18

Slip stitch (sl st), page 10

Bobble, page 15

INSTRUCTIONS

Potato Skin:

Rnd 1: With A and D-3 hook, make an adjustable ring, ch 1, 6 sc in ring. Pull tail to close ring—6 sts. Do not join at end of each round until instructed. Place marker at beginning of round and move marker up as each round is completed.

Rnd 2: 2 sc in each st around—12 sts.

Rnd 3: *2 sc in next st, sc in next st; rep from * around—18 sts.

Rnd 4: *2 sc in next st, sc in next 2 sts; rep from * around—24 sts.

Rnds 5–16: Sc in each st around.

Rnd 17: *Sc2tog, sc in next 2 sts; rep from * around—18 sts.

Rnd 18: *Sc2tog, sc in next st; rep from * around—12 sts.

- Place last stitch on marker to prevent unraveling. Stuff firmly with fiberfill and insert scent.

Rnd 19: [Sc2tog] around; join with sl st in first sc—6 sts.

- Fasten off, leaving a long tail. Weave end yarn tail through last round and pull gently to close.

Inside of Potato:

Row 1 (RS): With B and D-3 hook, ch 6, sc in 2nd ch from hook and in each ch across—5 sts.

Row 2: Ch 1, turn, 2 sc in first st, bobble [4 dc] in next st, sc in next 2 sts, 2 sc in last st—7 sts.

Row 3: Ch 1, turn, sc in each st across.

Row 4: Ch 1, turn, sc in first st, bobble [4 dc] in next st, sc in next 3 sts, bobble [4 dc] in next st, sc in last st.

Row 5: Rep Row 3.

Row 6: Ch 1, turn, sc in first 3 sts, bobble [4 dc] in next st, sc in last 3 sts.

Rows 7–10: Rep Rows 3–6.

Row 11: Rep Row 3.

Row 12: Ch 1, turn, sc2tog, sc in next 3 sts, sc2tog—5 sts.

- Fasten off and weave in ends. Make sure all bobbles are pushed out to the right side.

Rnd 13: With RS facing, join A with sl st in any corner; working in ends of rows and across top and bottom edges, evenly space 26 sl sts around; join with sl st in first st—27 sts.

Rnd 14: Ch 1, turn, sc in each st around; join with sl st in first st.

- Fasten off, leaving an 18-inch (45.5 cm) tail. Pin the inside of the potato to the potato skin and sew in place with yarn tail. Weave tail to the outside of the potato. With A, stitch short vertical stitches through the potato in a few spots on each side, pulling tightly to create small dimples. Knot the tail and weave back into the potato.

Butter:

Row 1 (RS): With C and C-2 hook, ch 4, sc in 2nd ch from hook and in each ch across—3 sts.

Rows 2 and 3: Ch 1, turn, sc in each st across.

- Fasten off, leaving a long tail. Use the tail and yarn needle to sew the butter to the center of the inside of the potato. Weave in ends.

Finishing:

- To add shredded cheese, straight-stitch orange yarn over the top of the potato and weave in ends. Bacon bits can be made by gluing dark red felt pieces into place. Glue tiny green pieces of felt on top for chives.

steak

For a nice dinner, a T-bone steak tops the list. Crochet this one in a shade of brown that matches how you like your steak cooked. Stuffed with a little steak seasoning, it will smell like it's fresh from the grill. One more trick for a realistic steak? Add grill marks with a dark brown or black permanent marker.

INSTRUCTIONS

Steak:

FIRST LAYER:

Row 1 (RS): With A, ch 15, sc in 2nd ch from hook and in each ch across—14 sts.

Row 2: Ch 1, turn, 2 sc in first st, sc in next 12 sts, 2 sc in last st—16 sts.

Rows 3–4: Ch 1, turn, sc in each st across.

Row 5: Ch 1, turn, [sc2tog] twice, sc in next 10 sts, sc2tog—13 sts.

Row 6: Ch 1, turn, sc2tog, sc in next 8 sts, sc2tog, sk last st—10 sts.

Row 7: Ch 1, turn, sc2tog, sc in next 6 sts, sc2tog—8 sts.

Row 8: Ch 1, turn, sc2tog, sc in last 6 sts—7 sts.

Row 9: Ch 1, turn, sc in each st across.

Row 10: Ch 1, turn, sc in first 2 sts, sc2tog, sc in last 3 sts—6 sts.

Rows 11–13: Ch 1, turn, sc in each st across.

Row 14: Ch 1, turn, sc in first 2 sts, sc2tog, sc in last 2 sts—5 sts.

Row 15: Ch 1, turn, sc2tog, sc in next st, sc2tog—3 sts.

Rnd 16: Ch 1; working in ends of rows and across top and bottom edges, evenly space 49 sc around; join with sl st in first st—49 sts.

- Fasten off.

SECOND LAYER:

Rows 1–15: Rep Rows 1–15 of first layer.

Rnd 16: Ch 1; working in ends of rows and across top and bottom edges, evenly space 49 sc around—49 sts. Do not join at end of each round until instructed. Place stitch marker at beginning of round and move marker up as each round is completed.

Rnd 17: Working in BLO, sc in each st around.

Rnd 18: Working in both loops, sc in each st around; join with sl st in first st.

MATERIALS AND TOOLS

Brown worsted weight yarn (A) ④

Tan worsted weight yarn (B) ④

Crochet hook: 3.25 mm (size D-3 U.S.)

Stitch marker

Yarn needle

Polyester fiberfill

Scent sachet: steak seasoning, page 7

Dark brown or black permanent marker

STITCHES AND TECHNIQUES USED

Chain stitch (ch), page 9

Single crochet (sc), page 10

Single crochet two together (sc2tog), page 18

Slip stitch (sl st), page 10

Back loops only (BLO), page 19

- Fasten off, leaving a long tail.

- Hold the steak layers with wrong sides together and sew together with the yarn tail. Insert the fiberfill and scent before completing the sewing. Weave in ends.

Bone (Make 2):

Row 1 (RS): With B, ch 13, sc in 2nd ch from hook and in next 5 chs; ch 8, sl st in 2nd ch from hook and in next 2 chs; sc in next 4 chs; working in foundation chain, sc in last 6 chs—19 sts.

- Fasten off, leaving a long tail.

- Repeat for a second bone.

- Sew a bone to each side of the steak. Weave in ends.

Finishing:

- With the permanent marker, draw parallel diagonal lines across the steak for grill marks.

iced tea

If you live in the South, a cold glass of iced tea with a lemon slice is the standard drink served with dinner. This pattern is easily adaptable, so if you'd rather have fruit punch, soda, or anything else, just change the color and scent. See the Drink Menu on the next page for ideas.

MATERIALS AND TOOLS

Light brown (or color of your choice) worsted weight yarn (A) 🔢

Light gray worsted weight yarn (B) 🔢

Light yellow worsted weight yarn (C) 🔢

Medium yellow worsted weight yarn (D) 🔢

Crochet hook: 3.25 mm (size D-3 U.S.)

Stitch marker

Yarn needle

Polyester fiberfill

Scent sachet: tea, lemon, or any scent of your choice, pages 6–7

STITCHES AND TECHNIQUES USED

Adjustable ring, page 11

Chain stitch (ch), page 9

Single crochet (sc), page 10

Back loops only (BLO), page 19

Single crochet two together (sc2tog), page 18

Slip stitch (sl st), page 10

Front loops only (FLO), page 19

Reverse single crochet (reverse sc), page 11

INSTRUCTIONS

Tea:

Rnd 1: With A, make an adjustable ring, ch 1, 6 sc in ring. Pull tail to close ring—6 sts. Do not join at end of each round until instructed. Place stitch marker at beginning of round and move marker up as each round is completed.

Rnd 2: 2 sc in each st around—12 sts.

Rnd 3: *2 sc in next st, sc in next st; rep from * around—18 sts.

Rnd 4: *2 sc in next st, sc in next 2 sts; rep from * around—24 sts.

Rnd 5: Working in BLO, sc in each st around.

Rnds 6–12: Working in both loops, sc in each st around.

Rnd 13: Working in BLO, *sc2tog, sc in next 2 sts; repeat from * around—18 sts.

Rnd 14: Working in both loops, *sc2tog, sc in next st; repeat from * around—12 sts.

- Place last stitch on stitch marker to prevent unraveling. Stuff with fiberfill and insert scent.

Rnd 15: [Sc2tog] around; join with sl st in first sc—6 sts.

- Fasten off and weave in ends.

Glass Rim:

Rnd 1: Working in unworked front loops of Rnd 13, join B with sc in any st; sc in each remaining st around—24 sts. Do not join at end of each round until instructed. Place stitch marker at beginning of round and move marker up as each round is completed.

Rnds 2 and 3: Working in both loops, sc in each st around.

Rnd 4: Ch 1, reverse sc in each st around; join with sl st in first sc.

- Fasten off and weave in ends.

Lemon Slice Layer (Make 2):

Rnd 1 (RS): With C, make an adjustable ring, ch 1, 6 sc in ring. Pull tail to close ring—6 sts.

Rnd 2: Ch 1, turn, 2 sc in each st—12 sts.

- Fasten off.

Rnd 3: With RS facing, join D with sl st in first st of Rnd 2; sl st in each st across.

- Fasten off.

- Repeat for a second lemon slice layer, but leave a long yarn tail.

- Weave end tail through first st to join invisibly. With wrong sides of the lemon slice layers held together, sew together with the end tail; then position the slice on rim of glass and sew in place with D yarn tail. Weave in ends.

Drink Menu

FLAVOR	DRINK COLOR (A)	SLICE COLOR (C AND D)	SCENT
Lemonade	Yellow or pink	Light yellow/Yellow	Lemon
Limeade	Green	Light green/Green	Lime
Fruit punch	Red	Light orange/Orange	Any fruit (berry, orange)
Cola	Brown	Light green/Green	Cola
Root beer	Brown	Light yellow/Yellow	Root beer
Lemon-lime soda	White	Light green/Green	Lemon or lime

salad

I love a nice salad, which can sometimes be a meal on its own, especially a leafy green crocheted one. Use as many shades of green as you want and stuff the tomatoes with some herbs or other seasoning to scent. Serve chilled, with dressing on the side, of course.

INSTRUCTIONS

Large Salad Leaf (Make 4 or more):

Row 1 (RS): With A, ch 14, dc in 3rd ch from hook and in next 8 chs, tr in last 3 chs —12 sts.

Row 2: Ch 3, turn, tr in first 3 sts, dc in last 9 sts.

Row 3: Ch 3, turn, working in BLO, dc in next 9, tr in last 3 sts.

Row 4: Rep Row 2.

- Fasten off and weave in ends.

- Repeat for additional large salad leaves.

Small Salad Leaf (Make 3 or more):

Row 1 (RS): With A, ch 10, dc in 3rd ch from hook and in next 5 chs, tr in last 2 chs —8 sts.

Row 2: Ch 3, turn, working in BLO, tr in first 2 sts, dc in last 6 sts.

- Fasten off and weave in ends.

- Repeat for additional small salad leaves.

Cherry Tomato (Make 3 or more):

Rnd 1: With B, make an adjustable ring, ch 1, 6 sc in ring. Pull tail to close ring— 6 sts. Do not join at end of each round until instructed. Place stitch marker at beginning of round and move marker up as each round is completed.

Rnd 2: *2 sc in next st, sc in next st; rep from * around—9 sts.

Rnds 3–4: Sc in each st around.

- Place last stitch on stitch marker to prevent unraveling. Stuff with fiberfill and insert scent.

Rnd 5: *Sc2tog, sc in next st; rep from * around; join with sl st in first sc—6 sts.

- Fasten off. Weave in ends.

- Repeat for additional cherry tomatoes.

- Toss salad leaves and tomatoes together and serve.

MATERIALS AND TOOLS

Green worsted weight yarn in one or more shades (A) (4)

Red worsted weight yarn (B) (4)

Crochet hook: 3.25 mm (size D-3 U.S.)

Stitch marker

Yarn needle

Polyester fiberfill

Scent sachet: ranch seasoning or various herbs, pages 6–7

STITCHES AND TECHNIQUES USED

Chain stitch (ch), page 9

Double crochet (dc), page 13

Treble crochet (tr), page 14

Back loops only (BLO), page 19

Adjustable ring, page 11

Single crochet (sc), page 10

Single crochet two together (sc2tog), page 18

sweet treats

I know we aren't supposed to eat sugar. I know it's really bad for you. Sugar causes all kinds of health problems, and doctors tell us we are all addicted to it. Well, isn't it nice we can just crochet all the sugary snacks we want? From ice cream that will never melt to cookies that never become stale, crocheted sweets are some of my favorites to make. They're fun to scent too, and the smells you'll want to use are so easy to find.

ice cream

Choose your favorite flavor, and you'll definitely find a yarn to match. Chocolate, vanilla, strawberry, mint chocolate chip, or anything at all—there's a scoop for you! Crochet a few and stack them up on a cone, or lay them side by side in a dish. Scented sweetly, they will make all your ice cream wishes come true.

Skill Level:
EASY

INSTRUCTIONS

Ice Cream Scoop:

Rnd 1: With A, make an adjustable ring, ch 1, 6 sc in ring. Pull tail to close ring— 6 sts. Do not join at end of each round until instructed. Place stitch marker at beginning of round and move marker up as each round is completed.

Rnd 2: 2 sc in each st around—12 sts.

Rnd 3: *2 sc in next st, sc in next st; rep from * around—18 sts.

Rnd 4: *Sc in next st, 2 sc in next st, sc in next st; rep from * around—24 sts.

Rnds 5–9: Sc in each st around.

Rnd 10: Working in BLO, *sc2tog, sc in next 2 sts; rep from * around—18 sts.

Rnd 11: Working in both loops, *sc2tog, sc in next st; rep from * around—12 sts.

- Place last stitch on stitch marker to prevent unraveling. Stuff with fiberfill and insert scent, leaving the last few rounds unstuffed so the bottom remains flat.

Rnd 12: [Sc2tog] around; join with sl st in first sc—6 sts. Fasten off, leaving a long tail.

Edging round: Join A with sl st in any unworked front loops of Rnd 9, *3 hdc in next st, sl st in next st; rep from * around, working last sl st in first sl st.

- Fasten off. Weave end tail of ice cream scoop through last round and pull gently to close.

- If desired, repeat for additional ice cream scoops.

Cone:

Rnds 1–3: With B, work same as Rnds 1–3 of Ice Cream Scoop.

Rnd 4: Working in BLO, sc in each st around.

Rnds 5–10: Working in both loops, sc in each st around.

Rnd 11: Working in FLO, *2 sc in next st, sc in next 2 sts; rep from * around—24 sts.

Rnds 12–17: Rep Rnds 4–9.

MATERIALS AND TOOLS

Worsted weight yarn in one or more ice cream colors of your choice, such as brown, off-white, pink, or light green (A) **(4)**

Golden yellow worsted weight yarn (B) **(4)**

Sport weight yarn for sauce in color(s) of your choice (optional)

Crochet hook: 3.25 mm (size D-3 U.S.)

Stitch marker

Yarn needle

Embroidery needle

Polyester fiberfill

Black embroidery floss or colored embroidery floss for sprinkles

Scent sachet: chocolate, vanilla, strawberry, or mint, pages 6–7

- - - - - - - - - - - - - - - - - -

Rnd 18: Working in BLO, *sc2tog, sc in next 2 sts; rep from * around—18 sts.

- Place last stitch on stitch marker to prevent unraveling. Stuff bottom only (up to Rnd 12) with fiberfill.

Rnd 19: *Sc2tog, sc in next st; rep from * around—12 sts.

Rnd 20: [Sc2tog] around; join with sl st in first sc—6 sts.

- Fasten off. To form the top portion of the cone, push Rnds 18–20 of the cone down into the inside. With B and a yarn needle, secure the inside of the cone to the sides of cone by working straight stitches around Rnd 11. Weave in ends.

- The sides of the cone will be formed from Rnds 5–17. Referring to the photo on the previous page and beginning at the bottom of the cone, embroider long diagonal lines with a strand of B and a yarn needle, five rows wide, in one direction as follows: insert needle from wrong side to right side between any 2 stitches of Rnd 5, *skip next 5 stitches, insert needle to wrong side between the next 2 corresponding stitches of Rnd 17, skip next 2 stitches of Rnd 5, insert needle from wrong side to right side between next 2 stitches; repeat from * around. When you've made the first set of diagonal lines around the cone, make a second set of diagonal stitches in the opposite direction to complete the crisscross design. Weave in ends.

Finishing:

- If you'd like to permanently attach ice cream scoops to the cone, use matching yarn and a yarn needle to stitch the edge of each scoop around the outside edge of the cone. Stack more scoops on top and stitch into place with matching yarn. Weave in ends.

- With black or brown embroidery floss and embroidery needle, work short stitches randomly on the scoop for chocolate sprinkles. For rainbow sprinkles, use scraps of colorful embroidery floss or a variegated yarn instead.

- To top your ice cream with sauce, work the Syrup pattern on page 37 in golden yellow for caramel, dark brown for hot fudge, or red for strawberry. Tack the edges of the sauce down to secure into place.

cake

When I was little, I remember being at birthday parties where there was the birthday cake with giant icing flowers that everyone wanted. This big ol' slice of cake has two layers, lots of icing, and a cute rose on top. You can crochet your cake, but don't eat it too (because, you know, yarn). Scent it with chocolate for red velvet or chocolate cake, or vanilla, or coconut, or strawberry (see the Cake Menu on the next page for suggestions). The delicious possibilities are endless!

MATERIALS AND TOOLS

Worsted weight yarn in icing color of your choice (A) ④

Worsted weight yarn in cake color of your choice (B) ④

Rose worsted weight yarn (C) ④

Light green worsted weight yarn (D) ④

Crochet hook: 3.25 mm (size D-3 U.S.)

Stitch marker

Yarn needle

Polyester fiberfill

Scent sachet: chocolate, vanilla, coconut, strawberry, or scent of your choice, pages 6–7

INSTRUCTIONS

Icing:

Row 1 (WS): Beginning at point of cake slice, with A, ch 3, 2 hdc in 3rd ch from hook—2 sts.

Row 2 (RS): Ch 2, turn, 2 hdc in each st across—4 sts.

Row 3: Ch 2, turn, hdc in each st across.

Row 4: Ch 2, turn, 2 hdc in first st, hdc in next 2 sts, 2 hdc in last st—6 sts.

Row 5: Ch 2, turn, 2 hdc in first st, hdc in next 4 sts, 2 hdc in last st—8 sts.

Row 6: Ch 2, turn, 2 hdc in first st, hdc in next 6 sts, 2 hdc in last st—10 sts.

Row 7: Ch 2, turn, hdc in each st across.

Row 8: Ch 2, turn, 2 hdc in first st, hdc in next 8 sts, 2 hdc in last st—12 sts.

Row 9: Ch 2, turn, hdc in each st across.

Row 10 (edging): Ch 1, *working in ends of rows, evenly space 16 sc across*, 3 sc in opposite side of foundation chain; rep from * to * to Row 9, ch 1, (bobble [5 dc], sl st) in each st across Row 9 to last st, bobble [5 dc] in last st—35 sc, 12 bobbles, 1 ch-1 sp. Do not turn.

Row 11 (RS): Working in BLO and in same direction as last row, sc in first 16 sts, sc2tog in next 2 sts, sc2tog in last stitch worked and in next st, sc in next 16 sts, hdc in ch-1 sp, hdc in each bobble [5 dc] across—47 sts.

Row 12: Ch 2, turn, hdc in first 13 sts across; leave remaining sts unworked—13 sts.

Rows 13–17: Ch 2, turn, hdc in each st across.

- Fasten off, leaving a long tail.

Cake:

Row 1 (RS): With RS facing and working in unworked front loops of Row 10 for Icing, join B with hdc in first st, hdc in next 15 sts, sc2tog, hdc in last 16 sts—33 sts.

Row 2: Ch 2, turn, hdc in each st across. Fasten off.

Row 3: With RS of Row 2 facing, join A with hdc in first st, hdc in each remaining st across. Fasten off.

Row 4: With WS of Row 3 facing, join B with hdc in last st, hdc in each remaining st across.

Row 5: Ch 2, turn, hdc in each st.

- Fasten off, leaving a long tail.

Bottom of Cake:

Rows 1–9: With B, rep Rows 1–9 of Icing.

- Fasten off, leaving a long tail. Sew the edges of the back of the icing and the cake together. Align the bottom of the cake with the lower edge of the icing and cake and sew together, stuffing with fiberfill and inserting scent as the work progresses.

Rose:

- With C, ch 18, 2 dc in 4th ch from hook and in each ch across to last ch, (sc, sl st) in last ch—15 sts.

- Fasten off, leaving a long tail. Roll up the rose and sew through all the rose layers at the bottom of the rose, securing the rose spiral together.

Leaf:

- With D, ch 4, sc in 2nd ch from hook, hdc in next ch, 6 dc in last ch; working in opposite side of foundation chain, hdc in next ch, sc in last ch, sl st in beginning ch—12 sts.

- Fasten off, leaving a long tail to sew the leaf to the icing. Use the rose tail to sew the rose to the icing, overlapping the leaf.

- Weave in ends.

STITCHES AND TECHNIQUES USED

Chain stitch (ch), page 9

Half double crochet (hdc), page 13

Single crochet (sc), page 10

Bobble stitch, page 15

Slip stitch (sl st), page 10

Single crochet two together (sc2tog), page 18

Back loops only (BLO), page 19

Front loops only (FLO), page 19

Crocheting into chain spaces (ch-sp), page 17

Cake Menu

FLAVOR	ICING COLOR (A)	CAKE COLOR (B)	SCENT
Chocolate	Dark brown	Brown	Chocolate
Vanilla	White	Ivory or yellow	Vanilla
Red Velvet	White or color of your choice	Red	Chocolate
Lemon	White	Yellow	Lemon
Carrot	Ivory	Light brown	Cinnamon
Coconut	White	Ivory	Coconut
Rainbow	White or color of your choice	Variegated	Vanilla
Strawberry	White or color of your choice	Pink	Strawberry

pie

A slice of pie and a cup of coffee are what diner dreams are made of. This pattern has instructions for customizing your slice. You can choose a smooth filling (chocolate, lemon, or coconut) or a lumpy filling (cherry, apple, or berries). Don't forget to add a meringue topping or a top crust. The meringue and top crust topping patterns can even be made in different colors so you can make one-crust pies like pumpkin, pecan, or strawberry (see Pie Menu on page 113). Your pie can be scented with any matching fragrance to make it so realistic you'll want to dig in as soon as you work the last stitch!

Skill Level:
INTERMEDIATE

INSTRUCTIONS

Bottom Crust:

Row 1 (WS): Beginning at point of pie, with A, ch 3, 2 hdc in 3rd ch from hook— 2 sts.

Row 2 (RS): Ch 2, turn, 2 hdc in each st across—4 sts.

Row 3: Ch 2, turn, hdc in each st across.

Row 4: Ch 2, turn, 2 hdc in first st, hdc in next 2 sts, 2 hdc in last st—6 sts.

Row 5: Ch 2, turn, 2 hdc in first st, hdc in next 4 sts, 2 hdc in last st—8 sts.

Row 6: Ch 2, turn, 2 hdc in first st, hdc in next 6 sts, 2 hdc in last st—10 sts.

Row 7: Ch 2, turn, hdc in each st across.

Row 8: Ch 2, turn, 2 hdc in first st, hdc in next 8 sts, 2 hdc in last st—12 sts.

Row 9: Ch 2, turn, hdc in each st across.

Row 10: Ch 1; working in same direction as Row 9, *work in ends of rows, evenly space 15 sc across*, 3 sc in opposite side of foundation chain; rep from * to *; leave remaining sts unworked—33 sc.

Row 11: Ch 1, turn, working in BLO, sc in each st across.

Row 12: Ch 1, working in same direction as Row 11 and in BLO of Row 9, evenly space 14 hdc across, sl st in first sc of Row 11.

Row 13: Ch 2, turn, 2 hdc in first st, hdc in next 12 sts, 2 hdc in last st—16 sts.

Rows 14–16: Ch 2, turn, hdc in each st across.

Row 17: Ch 1, turn, sk first st, 5 dc in next st, sk next st, sl st in next st, *sk next st, 5 dc in next st, sk next st, sl st in next st; rep from * across.

- Fasten off, leaving a long tail.

MATERIALS AND TOOLS

Tan worsted weight yarn (A) **4**

Worsted weight yarn in filling color of your choice (B) **4**

Off-white worsted weight yarn (C) **4**

Crochet hook: 3.25 mm (size D-3 U.S.)

Stitch marker

Yarn needle

Polyester fiberfill

Scent sachet: chocolate, lemon, coconut, cherry, apple, or berry, pages 6–7

Brown eye shadow or chalk (optional)

STITCHES AND TECHNIQUES USED

Chain stitch (ch), page 9

Half double crochet (hdc), page 13

Single crochet (sc), page 10

Back loops only (BLO), page 19

Slip stitch (sl st), page 10

Double crochet (dc), page 13

Changing color, page 20

Bobble stitch, page 15

Front loops only (FLO), page 19

Filling:

Time to fill your pie! Choose a smooth filling for a custard or cream pie, or a lumpy filling for fruit or berry pies.

SMOOTH FILLING:

Row 1: With RS of Row 11 of bottom crust facing and working in BLO, join B with sc in first st; sc in each remaining st—33 sts.

Rows 2–5: Ch 1, turn, sc in each st across.

- Fasten off and weave in ends.

LUMPY FILLING:

Rows 1–5: Work same as Rows 1–5 of Smooth Filling in Row 11 of bottom crust, adding bobbles [5 dc] randomly throughout the rows.

- Fasten off, leaving a long tail.

Pie Topping:

Top your pie however you'd like it. While I may not be able to make a successful meringue in real life (seriously, what am I doing wrong?), a crocheted meringue never fails. A smooth top crust is another alternative if you'd like a buttery, flaky crust.

MERINGUE TOPPING:

Row 1 (RS): Beginning at point of topping with C, ch 3, 2 hdc in 3rd ch from hook—2 sts.

Row 2: Ch 2, turn, 2 hdc in first st, (bobble [5 dc], hdc) in last st—4 sts.

Row 3: Ch 2, turn, hdc in first st, bobble [5 dc] in next st, hdc in last 2 sts.

Row 4: Ch 2, turn, (bobble [5 dc], hdc) in first st, hdc in next 2 sts, (bobble [5 dc], hdc) in last st—6 sts.

Row 5: Ch 2, turn, (bobble [5 dc], hdc) in first st, hdc in next 2 sts, bobble [5 dc] in next st, hdc in next st, 2 hdc in last st—8 sts.

Row 6: Ch 2, turn, 2 hdc in first st, bobble [5 dc] in next st, hdc in next 3 sts, bobble [5 dc] in next st, hdc in next st, 2 hdc in last st—10 sts.

Row 7: Ch 2, turn, bobble [5 dc] in first st, *hdc in next 3 sts, bobble [5 dc] in next st; rep from * across, hdc in last st.

Row 8: Ch 2, turn, (bobble [5 dc], hdc) in first st, hdc in next 2 sts, bobble [5 dc] in next st, hdc in next 3 sts, bobble [5 dc] in next st, hdc in next st, 2 hdc in last st—12 sts.

Row 9: Ch 2, turn, bobble [5 dc] in first st, hdc in next 3 sts, *bobble [5 dc] in next st, hdc in next 3 sts; rep from * across.

Rnd 10: Ch 1, working in same direction as previous row and *working in ends of rows, evenly space 16 sc across side* to point, 3 sc in opposite side of foundation chain; rep from * to * to top of piece, ch 1, sc in each st across; join with sl st in first st—47 sts.

Rnd 11: Working in BLO, ch 1, hdc in first 34 sts, sc in last 13 st; join with sl st in first st.

Row 12: Hdc in next 32 sts, sl st in next st; leave remaining sts unworked—33 sts.

- Fasten off, leaving a long tail.

TOP CRUST:

Row 1: Beginning at point of crust, with A, ch 3, 2 hdc in 3rd ch from hook—2 sts.

Row 2: Ch 2, turn, 2 hdc in each st across—4 sts.

Row 3: Ch 2, turn, hdc in each st across.

Row 4: Ch 2, turn, 2 hdc in first st, hdc in next 2 sts, 2 hdc in last st—6 sts.

Row 5: Ch 2, turn, 2 hdc in first st, hdc in next 4 sts, 2 hdc in last st—8 sts.

Row 6: Ch 2, turn, 2 hdc in first st, hdc in next 6 sts, 2 hdc in last st—10 sts.

Row 7: Ch 2, turn, hdc in each st across.

Row 8: Ch 2, turn, 2 hdc in first st, hdc in next 8 sts, 2 hdc in last st—12 sts.

Row 9: Ch 2, turn, hdc in each st across.

Row 10 (edging): Ch 1, working in same direction as previous row and *working in ends of rows, evenly space 16 sc across side* to point, 3 sc in opposite side of foundation chain; repeat from * to * to top of piece, sl st in next st—35 sts.

Row 11: Ch 2, turn, working in FLO, hdc in first 16 sts, sk next st, (2 hdc, ch 1, 2 hdc) in next st, sk next st, hdc in last 16 sts—36 sts, 1 ch-1 sp.

- Fasten off, leaving a long tail.

Assembly:

- With yarn tails, sew the edges of the filling to the back of the bottom crust.

- Align the edges of the topping of your choice and filling and sew together with yarn tails. If using the top crust, sew to filling, lining up the unworked back loops of Row 10 with the edge of the filling and stitching them together. Stuff and insert scent as you close up the last several stitches. Weave in ends.

Finishing:

- "Toast" the meringue by applying brown eye shadow or chalk color to each bobble with your fingertip or a cotton swab.

Pie Menu

FLAVOR	FILLING TYPE/COLOR	TOPPING/COLOR	SCENT
Chocolate Mousse	Smooth/Brown	Meringue/White	Chocolate
Lemon Meringue	Smooth/Yellow	Meringue/White	Lemon
Cherry	Lumpy/Red	Top Crust/Tan	Cherry
Blueberry	Lumpy/Dark blue	Top Crust/Tan	Blueberry
Key Lime	Smooth/Lime green	Meringue/White	Lime
Coconut Cream	Smooth/Ivory	Meringue/White	Coconut
Pumpkin	Smooth/Dark orange	Top Crust/Dark orange	Pumpkin pie spice
Apple	Lumpy/Gold	Top Crust/Tan	Apple or Cinnamon
Banana Cream	Lumpy/Light yellow	Meringue/White	Banana or Vanilla
Pecan	Smooth/Gold	Meringue/Dark brown	Pecan or Maple
Strawberry	Lumpy/Red	Meringue/Red	Strawberry

chocolate bar

When no other dessert will do, a simple bar of chocolate always satisfies. This one is complete with a torn-away wrapper, so you won't get your hands messy. Add felt lettering to the label for a realistic look. Prefer white chocolate? Substitute a creamy off-white yarn for the dark brown yarn.

Skill Level:
EASY

INSTRUCTIONS

Chocolate Bar:

Rnd 1: With A, ch 9, sc in 2nd ch from hook and in next 6 chs, 3 sc in last ch; working in opposite side of foundation chain, sc in next 7 chs, 3 sc in beg ch—20 sts. Do not join at end of each round until instructed. Place marker at beginning of round and move marker up as each round is completed.

Rnds 2 and 3: Sc in each st around; then change color to B at end of Rnd 3.

Rnd 4: Sl st in each st around.

Rnds 5–16: Sc in each st around; then change color to A.

Rnd 17: Sl st in each st around.

Rnd 18: Sc in each st around; then change color to C.

Rnd 19: Working in BLO, sc in each st around.

Rnds 20–24: Working in both loops, sc in each st around; at end of last rnd, join with sl st in first sc.

- Fasten off, leaving a long tail. Stuff chocolate bar with fiberfill and insert scent.

- Flatten chocolate bar and sew stitches of top edge together with yarn tail.

Wrapper Edge:

Rnd 1: Working in FLO, join A with sc in any st of Rnd 18 of chocolate bar, sc in each st around—20 sts. Do not join.

Rnd 2: Sc in next 10 sts, 2 hdc in next st, 3 dc in next st, 2 hdc in next st, sl st in next st, 3 hdc in next st, 2 sc in next st, sc in next 4 sts; join with sl st in first sc—27 sts.

- Fasten off. Weave in ends.

Finishing:

- Cut white felt letters to spell part of *CHOCOLATE*; only make enough letters to fit across the wrapper, as shown in the photo. Depending on the size of the letters, you may need more or fewer letters than shown in the photo. Glue each letter into place.

- With a strand of C, embroider a grid pattern on the chocolate using back stitch, if desired.

MATERIALS AND TOOLS

Silver or gray worsted weight yarn (A) **4**

Red worsted weight yarn (B) **4**

Dark brown worsted weight yarn (C) **4**

Crochet hook: 3.25 mm (size D-3 U.S.)

Stitch marker

Yarn needle

Polyester fiberfill

Scent sachet: chocolate, page 6

White felt

Gel formula cyanoacrylate glue or craft glue

STITCHES AND TECHNIQUES USED

Chain stitch (ch), page 9

Single crochet (sc), page 10

Slip stitch (sl st), page 10

Changing color, page 20

Back loops only (BLO), page 19

Half double crochet (hdc), page 13

Front loops only (FLO), page 19

Double crochet (dc), page 13

cookies

Probably my favorite dessert, a cookie is just small enough so that you don't feel too guilty, but just big enough to satisfy your sweet tooth. This pattern is for a chocolate chip cookie. You can change the chip colors to make candy-coated chocolates, or leave them off for a plain sugar cookie. Make yours with a bite taken out, if you'd like. Scent with chocolate, vanilla, or any bakery aroma.

Skill Level:
EASY

INSTRUCTIONS

Whole Cookie Layer (Make 2):

Rnd 1: With A, make an adjustable ring, ch 1, 6 sc in ring. Pull tail to close ring—6 sts. Do not join at end of each round until instructed. Place marker at beginning of round and move marker up as each round is completed.

Rnd 2: 2 sc in each st around—12 sts.

Rnd 3: *2 sc in next st, sc in next st; rep from * around—18 sts.

Rnd 4: *Sc in next st, 2 sc in next st, sc in next st; rep from * around—24 sts.

Rnd 5: *2 sc in next st, sc in next 3 sts; rep from * around; join with sl st in first sc—30 sts.

- Fasten off, leaving a long tail.

- Repeat for a second whole cookie layer.

Bitten Cookie Layer (Make 2):

Rnds 1–3: Work same as Rnds 1–3 of whole cookie.

Rnd 4: *Sc in next st, 2 sc in next st, sc in next st*; rep from * to * twice, ch 1, sl st in next 3 sts, ch 1; rep from * to * twice—20 sc, 3 sl sts.

Rnd 5: *2 sc in next st, sc in next 3 sts*; rep from * to * twice, ch 2, sl st in last sc worked and next 3 sl sts, ch 2; rep from * to * twice; join with sl st in first sc—25 sts, 4 sl sts.

- Fasten off, leaving a long tail.

- Repeat for a second bitten cookie layer.

Assembly:

- Hold the matching layers together and sew around edges with the yarn tail, adding a bit of fiberfill and your chosen scent between the layers before completing. Weave in ends.

Finishing:

- Cut small irregular circles from brown felt for chocolate chips, or use the felt color of your choice for candy-coated chocolate. Glue or sew in place.

MATERIALS AND TOOLS

Light brown worsted weight yarn in (A) (4)

Crochet hook: 3.25 mm (size D-3 U.S.)

Stitch marker

Yarn needle

Polyester fiberfill

Scent sachet: chocolate, vanilla, or scent of your choice, pages 6–7

Brown felt for chocolate chips and colored felt for candy-coated chocolate

Craft glue or brown embroidery floss and embroidery needle

STITCHES AND TECHNIQUES USED

Adjustable ring, page 11

Chain stitch (ch), page 9

Single crochet (sc), page 10

Slip stitch (sl st), page 10

croissant

A buttery, flaky croissant is a delicious treat with a cup of tea or espresso. This crocheted croissant is made like the real ones. A big crocheted "pastry" triangle is rolled up and curved into a croissant shape. Tuck in a butter, bread, or soft vanilla scent, and finish the edges with light brown eye shadow or chalk to mimic the crispy toasted edges of the real thing.

INSTRUCTIONS

Row 1: Beginning at the tip of the triangle, with A, ch 2, 2 sc in 2nd ch from hook—2 sts.

Row 2 and all even-numbered rows up to Row 20: Ch 1, turn, sc in each st across.

Row 3: Ch 1, turn, sc in first st, 2 sc in last st—3 sts.

Row 5: Ch 1, turn, sc in first st, 2 sc in next st, sc in last st—4 sts.

Row 7: Ch 1, turn, sc in first 2 sts, 2 sc in next st, sc in last st—5 sts.

Row 9: Ch 1, turn, sc in first 2 sts, 2 sc in next st, sc in last 2 sts—6 sts.

Row 11: Ch 1, turn, sc in first 3 sts, 2 sc in next st, sc in last 2 sts—7 sts.

Row 13: Ch 1, turn, sc in first 3 sts, 2 sc in next st, sc in last 3 sts—8 sts.

Row 15: Ch 1, turn, sc in first 4 sts, 2 sc in next st, sc in last 3 sts—9 sts.

Row 17: Ch 1, turn, sc in first 4 sts, 2 sc in next st, sc in last 4 sts—10 sts.

Row 19: Ch 1, turn, sc in first 5 sts, 2 sc in next st, sc in last 4 sts—11 sts.

Row 21: Ch 1, turn, sc in first 5 sts, 2 sc in next st, sc in last 5 sts—12 sts.

Row 22: Ch 1, turn, sc in first 6 sts, 2 sc in next st, sc in last 5 sts—13 sts.

Row 23: Ch 1, turn, sc in first 6 sts, 2 sc in next st, sc in last 6 sts—14 sts.

Row 24: Ch 1, turn, sc in first 7 sts, 2 sc in next st, sc in last 6 sts—15 sts.

Rows 25–27: Ch 1, turn, 2 sc in first st, sc in each st across to last st, 2 sc in last st—21 sts.

Row 28: Ch 1, turn, sc in next 10 sts, 2 sc in next st, sc in last 10 sts—22 sts.

Rows 29–31: Repeat Row 2.

- Fasten off, leaving a long yarn tail. Beginning at Row 31, roll up the crocheted triangle, starting from the wide end. Tuck the scent in near the middle of the triangle. No stuffing is necessary. Pin the roll in place and with end tail of yarn, sew edges of croissant together, curving the rolled shape into a crescent and securing the point of the triangle in place. Weave in ends.

Finishing:

- With your fingertip or a cotton swab, "toast" the edges of the croissant layers with eye shadow or chalk.

MATERIALS AND TOOLS

Worsted weight yarn in tan (A) 〔4〕

Crochet hook: 3.25 mm (size D-3 U.S.)

Yarn needle

Embroidery needle

Straight pins

Scent sachet: butter, bread, or vanilla, pages 6–7

Brown eye shadow or chalk

STITCHES AND TECHNIQUES USED

Chain stitch (ch), page 9

Single crochet (sc), page 10

cinnamon roll

Hot, fresh cinnamon rolls with cream cheese icing make the whole house smell heavenly. This crocheted version with cinnamon scent inside smells like you've been baking all day.

INSTRUCTIONS

Row 1: With A, ch 49, sc in 2nd ch from hook and in next 47 chs—48 sts.

Rows 2–5: Ch 1, turn, sc in each st across; at end of last row, change color to B.

Row 6: Ch 1, turn, sl st in each st across.

Rows 7–11: Ch 1, turn, sc in each st across.

- Fasten off, leaving a long tail. Holding first and last rows together, sew the edges of the three open sides together, inserting the scent before completing the stitching. Roll the piece into a spiral (see photo) and with a strand of A, secure the layers together. Weave in ends.

Finishing:

- Cut an 18-inch (45.5 cm) strand of C. Squeeze a thin line of glue on the spiral of the cinnamon roll and press the strand to the glue to secure for icing. Trim excess yarn.

MATERIALS AND TOOLS

Tan worsted weight yarn (A) **4**

Brown worsted weight yarn (B) **4**

Off-white worsted weight yarn (C) **4**

Crochet hook: 3.25 mm (size D-3 U.S.)

Stitch marker

Yarn needle

Scent sachet: cinnamon, page 6

Craft glue

STITCHES AND TECHNIQUES USED

Chain stitch (ch), page 9

Single crochet (sc), page 10

Slip stitch (sl st), page 10

Changing color, page 20

extras

AmiguruME Eats are fun on their own, but add some plates, utensils, or a cute teapot, and you have a play food party! In this section, you'll learn how to make some cute little accessories to go with all the food you've made. They make the AmiguruME Eats experience even more realistic and offer an adorable way to display all your goodies.

lunch box

When I was little, a new school year meant picking out a new lunch box or dusting off my favorite from the year before. Now with kids of my own, I have to admit I was sad when they didn't want to use their character lunch boxes! This pattern creates a functional and basic lunch box that opens and closes. Plastic canvas makes the sides sturdy, and a button closure secures all your favorite AmiguruME Eats inside. The cute little handle is attached with D-rings for school lunch box realness!

INSTRUCTIONS

Lid:

Row 1: With A, ch 28, sc in 2nd ch from hook and in each ch across—27 sts.

Rows 2–21: Ch 1, turn, sc in each st across. Continue in unturned rounds. Do not join at end of each round until instructed. Place marker for beginning of round and move marker up as each round is completed.

Rnd 22: *Ch 2, working in ends of rows, evenly space 21 sts*; ch 2, working in opposite side of foundation chain, sc in next 27 chs of Row 1; rep from * to *; ch 2, sc in each st of Row 21—96 sts, 4 ch-2 sps.

Rnd 23: *2 sc in next ch-2 sp, sc in each st around to next ch-2 sp; rep from * around—104 sts.

Rnd 24: Working in BLO, *sc2tog, sc in next 21 sts, sc2tog, sc in next 27 sts; rep from * around—100 sts.

Rnds 25–27: Working in both loops, sc in each st around.

Rnd 28: Working in BLO, sc2tog, sc in next 20 sts, sc2tog, sc in next 26 sts, sc2tog, sc in next 19 sts, sc2tog, sc in next 27 sts—96 sts.

Rnds 29–31: Working in both loops, sc in each st around; join with sl st in first sc at end of last rnd.

- Fasten off, leaving an 18-inch (45.5 cm) tail. Thread the end tail on the yarn needle. Fold down Rnds 24–28 to form the lid's inside edge, and sew in place along the inside edge, working the needle through the folded layers. Weave in ends.

Box:

Row 1–Rnd 22: Work same as Rows 1 through Rnd 22 of Lid.

Rnd 23: Working in BLO, sc in each st around, working 1 sc in each ch-2 sp—100 sts.

Rnd 24: Working in both loops, *sc2tog, sc in next 20 sts, sc2tog, sc in next 26 sts; rep from * to end of rnd—96 sts.

Rnds 25–34: Sc in each st around.

Rnd 35: Working in BLO, *sc2tog, sc in next 18 sts, sc2tog, sc in next 26 sts; rep from * around—92 sts.

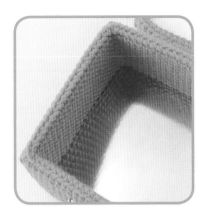

Rnds 36–45: Working in both loops, sc in each st around; join with sl st in first sc at end of last rnd.

- Fasten off, leaving an 18-inch (45.5 cm) tail.

Hinge Panel:

Row 1: With A, ch 21, sc in 2nd ch from hook and in each ch across—20 sts.

Rows 2–4: Ch 1, turn, sc in each st across.

- Fasten off, leaving a long tail. Place the lid on the box in a closed position. Pin the hinge panel in place along one of the long edges of the box and on the outside of the

lid. Thread the end tail on the yarn needle. Sew the hinge panel in place along its long edges. Weave in ends.

Handle:

Row 1: With B and leaving a long tail, ch 5, sc in 2nd ch from hook and in each ch across—4 sts.

Rows 2–29: Ch 1, turn, sc in each st across.

- Fasten off, leaving a long tail. Insert each end of the handle in a D-ring, fold the ends over the D-rings, then sew the ends to the handle with yarn. With a strand of B, sew the handle to the box on the side opposite from the hinge panel. Weave in ends.

Closure:

Row 1: With B, ch 18.

- Fasten off, leaving a long tail. Sew the closure onto the lid on the center of the long edge opposite the hinge panel.

Skill Level:
INTERMEDIATE

MATERIALS AND TOOLS

Worsted weight yarn in lunch box color of your choice (A) (4)

White worsted weight yarn for handle (B) (4)

Crochet hook: 3.25 mm (size D-3 U.S.)

Stitch marker

Yarn needle

Straight pins

Plastic canvas, 12 × 18 inches (30.5 × 45.5 cm)

Silver foil card stock or felt, 12-inch (30.5 cm) square

Gel formula cyanoacrylate glue

Two 1-inch (2.5 cm) metal D-rings

White 1-inch (2.5 cm) button

Sewing thread and needle (optional)

STITCHES AND TECHNIQUES USED

Chain stitch (ch), page 9

Single crochet (sc), page 10

Back loops only (BLO), page 19

Single crochet two together (sc2tog), page 18

Slip stitch (sl st), page 10

Crocheting into chain spaces (ch-sp), page 17

Finishing:

- For the lining of the lid, cut one piece of plastic canvas and silver foil card stock, each measuring 7 × 5¼ inches (18 × 13.5 cm). For the lining of the box bottom, cut one piece of plastic canvas and card stock, each measuring 6¾ × 5 inches (17 × 12.5 cm). Round the corners of each piece with scissors. Place the plastic canvas pieces in the lid and the bottom of the box. Sew each piece in place with a strand of A. Apply a small line of glue along the edges of card stock. Press the card stock in place onto the plastic canvas pieces on the lid and bottom of the box. If you prefer to use felt instead of card stock, sew it in place with a sewing needle and thread in a color that matches A.

- For the lining of the box sides, cut two pieces of plastic canvas measuring 2½ × 6¾ inches (6.4 × 17 cm) and two pieces measuring 2½ × 4¾ inches (6.4 ×12 cm). Line the inside of the box sides with the plastic canvas pieces, matching the long and short edges. Sew each piece in place with a strand of A. To finish forming the inside edges of the box, fold down Rnds 23–35 of the box. Thread the end tail on the yarn needle. Sew the folded rounds in place along the inside edges of the box, working the needle through the second layer to wrong side of box. Weave in ends.

- Position the button on the outside of the box so the closure loops over button; then sew the button in place with yarn.

place setting

If you're going to sit down and have an AmiguruME Eats meal, you will need a plate, a fork, and a spoon, of course. Choose any colors you'd like for your crocheted place setting. Best part: you'll never need to wash these dishes!

MATERIALS AND TOOLS

White worsted weight yarn (A) **4**

Red worsted weight yarn (or any trim color of your choice) (B) **4**

Gray worsted weight yarn (C) **4**

Crochet hook: 3.25 mm (size D-3 U.S.)

Stitch marker

Yarn needle

Plastic canvas, 12 × 18 inches (30.5 cm × 45.5 cm)

STITCHES AND TECHNIQUES USED

Adjustable ring, page 11

Chain stitch (ch), page 9

Single crochet (sc), page 10

Change color, page 20

Slip stitch (sl st), page 10

Single crochet two together (sc2tog), page 18

Back loops only (BLO), page 19

INSTRUCTIONS

Plate:

Rnd 1: With A, make an adjustable ring, ch 1, 6 sc in ring. Pull tail to close ring—6 sts. Do not join at end of each round until instructed. Place marker at beginning of round and move marker up as each round is completed.

Rnd 2: 2 sc in each st around—12 sts.

Rnd 3: *2 sc in next st, sc in next st; rep from * around—18 sts.

Rnd 4: *Sc in next st, 2 sc in next st, sc in next st; rep from * around—24 sts.

Rnd 5: *2 sc in next st, sc in next 3 sts; rep from * around—30 sts.

Rnd 6: *Sc in next st, 2 sc in next st, sc in next 3 sts; rep from * around—36 sts.

Rnd 7: *Sc in next 5 sts, 2 sc in next st; rep from * around—42 sts.

Rnd 8: *Sc in next 3 sts, 2 sc in next st, sc in next 3 sts; rep from * around—48 sts.

Rnd 9: *Sc in next 6 sts, 2 sc in next st, sc in next st; rep from * around—54 sts.

Rnd 10: *2 sc in next st, sc in next 8 sts; rep from * around; then change color to B—60 sts.

Rnd 11 (border rnd): Sl st in each st around; then change color to A—60 sl sts.

Rnd 12: *Sc in next 6 sts, 2 sc in next st, sc in next 3 sts; rep from * around—66 sts.

Rnd 13: *Sc in next 2 sts, 2 sc in next st, sc in next 8 sts; rep from * around—72 sts.

Rnd 14: Sc in each st around.

Rnd 15: *Sc2tog, sc in next 10 sts; rep from * around—66 sts.

Rnd 16: *Sc in next 5 sts, sc2tog, sc in next 4 sts; rep from * around—60 sts.

Rnd 17: *Sc in next st, sc2tog, sc in next 7 sts; rep from * around—54 sts.

Rnd 18: *Sc in next 7 sts, sc2tog; rep from * around—48 sts.

Rnd 19: *Sc2tog, sc in next 6 sts; rep from * around—42 sts.

Rnd 20: *Sc in next 3 sts, sc2tog, sc in next 2 sts; rep from * around—36 sts.

- Place last stitch on stitch marker to prevent unraveling. Flatten the plate and use as a template to cut a circle from the plastic canvas. Place the plastic canvas circle onto the plate. Hold the plastic canvas in place as you continue working the remaining rounds.

Rnd 21: *Sc in next st, sc2tog, sc in next 3 sts; rep from * around—30 sts.

Rnd 22: Sl st in each st around (to form a ring around bottom of plate).

Rnd 23: Working in BLO, *sc2tog, sc in next 3 sts; rep from * around—24 sts.

Rnd 24: Working in both loops, *sc in next st, sc2tog, sc in next st; rep from * around—18 sts.

Rnd 25: *Sc2tog, sc in next st; rep from * around—12 sts.

Rnd 26: [Sc2tog] around; join with sl st in first sc—6 sts.

- Fasten off, leaving a long tail. Weave tail through the last round, then pull gently to close.

Spoon:

BOWL OF SPOON:

Rnd 1: With C, make an adjustable ring, ch 1, 6 sc in ring. Pull tail to close ring—6 sts. Do not join at end of each round until instructed. Place marker at beginning of round and move marker up as each round is completed.

Rnd 2: 2 sc in each st around—12 sts.

Rnd 3: *2 sc in next st, sc in next 3 sts; rep from * around—15 sts.

Rnd 4: Sc in each st around.

Rnd 5: Working in BLO, sc in each st around.

Rnd 6: Working in both loops, *sc2tog, sc in next 3 sts; rep from * around—12 sts.

Rnd 7: [Sc2tog] around; join with sl st in first sc—6 sts.

- Fasten off. Weave in ends of head and flatten piece.

SPOON HANDLE:

Rnd 1: With C, make an adjustable ring, ch 1, 6 sc in ring. Pull tail to close ring—6 sts. Do not join at end of each round until instructed. Place marker at beginning of round and move marker up as each round is completed.

Rnd 2: *2 sc in next st, sc in next st; rep from * around—9 sts.

Rnds 3–4: Sc in each st around.

Rnd 5: Sc2tog, sc in each remaining st around—8 sts.

Rnds 6–8: Sc in each st around.

Rnd 9: Sc2tog, sc in each remaining st around—7 sts.

Rnds 10–12: Sc in each st around.

Rnd 13: Sc2tog, sc in each remaining st around—6 sts.

Rnds 14–15: Sc in each st around; join with sl st in first sc at end of last rnd.

- Fasten off, leaving a long tail. Cut a narrow ½ × 5½ inch (1.5 × 14 cm) piece of plastic canvas and insert into the handle. Sew the handle to the edge of the bowl of the spoon, working though both layers of each piece.

Fork:

TINES (MAKE 3):

Rnd 1: With C, make an adjustable ring, ch 1, 4 sc in ring. Pull tail to close ring—4 sts. Do not join at end of each round until instructed. Place marker at beginning of round and move marker up as each round is completed.

Rnds 2–4: Sc in each st around; join with sl st in first sc at end of last round.

- Fasten off, leaving a short tail. Tuck the tail in the tine before working the handle.

- Repeat Rnds 1–4 to make two more tines; do not join or cut yarn at the end of the last round of the last tine so that you can crochet the fork handle.

FORK HANDLE:

Rnd 5: Holding tines together with Rnd 4 facing and flattened with 2 sts visible on each side, sc in first 2 sts of 2nd tine, sc in each st of first tine, sc in last 2 sts of 2nd tine, sc in each st of last tine—12 sts. Do not join at end of each round until instructed. Place marker at beginning of round and move marker up as each round is completed.

Rnds 6–8: Sc in each st around.

Rnd 9: [Sc2tog] around—6 sts.

Rnd 10: Sc in each st around.

Rnd 11: 2 sc in next st, sc in each remaining st around—7 sts.

Rnds 12 and 13: Sc in each st around.

Rnd 14: 2 sc in next st, sc in each remaining st around—8 sts.

Rnds 15–17: Sc in each st around.

Rnd 18: 2 sc in next st, sc in each remaining st around—9 sts.

Rnds 19 and 20: Sc in each st around.

Rnd 21: *Sc2tog, sc in next st; rep from * around; join with sl st in first sc—6 sts.

- Fasten off, leaving a long tail. Weave the end tail through the last round and pull gently to close. Cut a narrow piece of plastic canvas measuring ½ × 5½ inches (1.5 × 14 cm) and insert into the handle.

teapot

For a proper afternoon tea, crochet this little teapot. The lid is removable and fits securely in place. You can even add a scent to make your tea party come to life.

MATERIALS AND TOOLS

Worsted weight yarn in teapot color of your choice (A) (4)

Brown worsted weight yarn (B) (4)

Polyester fiberfill

Crochet hook: 3.25 mm (size D-3 U.S.)

Stitch marker

Yarn needle

Embroidery needle (optional)

Straight pins

Pink, rose, and green embroidery floss (optional)

Scent sachet: tea, coffee, or scent of your choice, pages 6–7

- - - - - - - - - - - - - - - - - - - -

INSTRUCTIONS

Body of Teapot:

Rnd 1: With A, make an adjustable ring, ch 1, 6 sc in ring. Pull tail to close ring—6 sts. Do not join at end of each round until instructed. Place marker at beginning of round and move marker up as each round is completed.

Rnd 2: 2 sc in each st around—12 sts.

Rnd 3: *2 sc in next st, sc in next st; rep from * around—18 sts.

Rnd 4: *Sc in next st, 2 sc in next st, sc in next st; rep from * around—24 sts.

Rnd 5: Sl st in each st around (to form a ring on which the teapot will stand).

Rnd 6: Working in BLO, *2 sc in next st, sc in next 3 sts; rep from * around—30 sts.

Rnd 7: Working in both loops, *sc in next st, 2 sc in next st, sc in next 3 sts; rep from * around—36 sts.

Rnd 8: *Sc in next 5 sts, 2 sc in next st; rep from * around—42 sts.

Rnd 9: *Sc in next 6 sts, 2 sc in next st, sc in next 7 sts; rep from * around—45 sts.

Rnds 10–16: Sc in each st around.

Rnd 17: *Sc2tog, sc in next 13 sts; rep from * around—42 sts.

Rnd 18: *Sc in next 3 sts, sc2tog, sc in next 2 sts; rep from * around—36 sts.

Rnd 19: *Sc in next 4 sts, sc2tog; rep from * around—30 sts.

Rnd 20: *Sc2tog, sc in next 8 sts; rep from * around—27 sts.

Rnd 21: *Sc in next 3 sts, sc2tog, sc in next 4 sts; rep from * around—24 sts.

Rnd 22: Working in BLO, sc in each st around.

Rnd 23: Working in both loops, *2 sc in next st, sc in next 3 sts; rep from * around—30 sts.

Rnd 24: *Sc in next 2 sts, 2 sc in next st, sc in next 2 sts; rep from * around; change color to B—36 sts.

Rnd 25: Working in FLO, sc in each st around.

Rnd 26: Working in both loops, *sc2tog, sc in next 4 sts; rep from * around—30 sts.

Rnd 27: *Sc in next 2 sts, sc2tog, sc in next st; rep from * around—24 sts.

Rnd 28: *Sc2tog, sc in next 2 sts; rep from * around—18 sts. Place last stitch on stitch marker to prevent unraveling. Stuff teapot with fiberfill to Round 22 and insert scent.

Rnd 29: *Sc in next st, sc2tog; rep from * around—12 sts.

Rnd 30: [Sc2tog] around; join with sl st in first sc—6 sts.

- Fasten off, leaving a long tail. Weave tail through last round and pull gently to close. Push Rnds 25–30 down into the teapot to create the rim of the teapot and the "tea" inside.

Spout:

Rnd 1: Leaving a long tail for sewing, with A, make an adjustable ring, ch 1, 6 sc in ring. Pull tail to close ring—6 sts. Do not join at end of each round until instructed. Place marker at beginning of round and move marker up as each round is completed.

Rnd 2: 2 sc in each st around—12 sts.

Rnd 3: Working in BLO, sc in each st around.

Rnd 4: Working in both loops, sl st in next 6 sts, *2 dc in next st, dc in next st; rep from * around—15 sts.

Rnd 5: Sl st in next 6 sts, dc in next 9 sts.

Rnd 6: Sl st in next 6 sts, *hdc2tog, dc in next st; rep from * around—12 sts.

Rnd 7: Sc in each st around.

Rnd 8: *Sc2tog, sc in next 4 sts; rep from * around—10 sts.

Rnd 9: *Sc in next 2 sts, sc2tog, sc in next st; rep from * around—8 sts.

Rnds 10–14: Sc in each st around.

- Place last stitch on stitch marker to prevent unraveling and stuff the spout with fiberfill, leaving remaining rounds unstuffed.

- - - - - - - - - - - - - - - - -

Rnd 15: Working in BLO, sc in each st around.

Rnd 16: Working in both loops, [sc2tog] around; join with sl st in first sc—4 sts.

- Fasten off. Push Rnds 15 and 16 into the spout. Pin Rnds 1 and 2 to the teapot and sew in place with beginning yarn tail.

Lid:

Rnd 1: With A, make an adjustable ring, ch 1, 6 sc in ring. Pull tail to close ring—6 sts. Do not join at end of each round until instructed. Place marker at beginning of round and move marker up as each round is completed.

Rnd 2: 2 sc in each st around—12 sts.

Rnd 3: *2 sc in next st, sc in next st; rep from * around—18 sts.

Rnd 4: *Sc in next 3 sts, 2 sc in next st, sc in next 2 sts; rep from * around—21 sts.

Rnd 5: *Sc in next 6 sts, 2 sc in next st; rep from * around—24 sts.

Rnd 6: *Sc in next 2 sts, 2 sc in next st, sc in next 5 sts; rep from * around—27 sts.

Rnd 7: *Sc in next 8 sts, 2 sc in next st; rep from * around—30 sts.

Rnd 8: Working in BLO, *sc2tog, sc in next 3 sts; rep from * around—24 sts.

Rnd 9: Working in FLO, sc in each st around.

Rnd 10: Working in both loops, sc in each st around.

Rnd 11: Working in BLO, *sc2tog, sc in next st; rep from * around—18 sts.

- Place last stitch on stitch marker to prevent unraveling. Stuff the lid with fiberfill and insert scent.

Rnd 12: Working in both loops, *sc2tog, sc in next st; rep from * around—12 sts.

Rnd 13: [Sc2tog] around; join with sl st in first sc—6 sts.

- Fasten off, leaving a long tail. Weave tail through last round and pull gently to close.

Handle:

Rnd 1: With A, make an adjustable ring, ch 1, 6 sc in ring. Pull tail to close ring— 6 sts. Do not join at end of each round until instructed. Place marker at beginning of round and move marker up as each round is completed.

Rnds 2–17: Sc in each st around; join with sl st in first sc at end of last rnd.

- Fasten off, leaving a long tail. Referring to the photo on page 130 as a guide for placement, flatten and sew the handle to the body of the teapot on the side, opposite from the spout. Weave in ends.

Finishing:

- With the embroidery needle and embroidery floss, cross-stitch the rose pattern onto one or both sides of the teapot.

						X	X	X			
					X	X	X	X	X		X	X
				X	X	X	X	X	X	X	X	X	X
X				X	X	X	X	X	X	X	X	X
X	X			X	X	X	X	X	X	X	X
X	X	X		X	X	X	X	X	X	X
X	X	X	X	X	X	X	X	X	X
	X	X	X		X	X	X	X	X
		X	X	X	X	X	X	X
			X	X	X	X	X	X
		X	X	X
	X	X

ketchup & mustard bottles

If you're going to crochet things like French Fries (page 58) or a Hot Dog (page 51), you just can't leave out the all-important crocheted condiments! These little bottles of ketchup and mustard are the perfect accompaniment to your AmiguruME Eats table. Change the colors and labels to make any number of other sauces.

MATERIALS AND TOOLS

Red worsted weight yarn (A) (4)

Yellow worsted weight yarn (B) (4)

Crochet hook: 3.25 mm (size D-3 U.S.)

Stitch marker

Yarn needle

Polyester fiberfill

Black felt

Cyanoacrylate glue

STITCHES AND TECHNIQUES USED

Adjustable ring, page 11

Chain stitch (ch), page 9

Single crochet (sc), page 10

Back loops only (BLO), page 19

Single crochet two together (sc2tog), page 18

Slip stitch (sl st), page 10

INSTRUCTIONS

Rnd 1: With A (ketchup) or B (mustard), make an adjustable ring, ch 1, 6 sc in ring. Pull tail to close ring—6 sts. Do not join at end of each round until instructed. Place marker at beginning of round and move marker up as each round is completed.

Rnd 2: 2 sc in each st around—12 sts.

Rnd 3: *2 sc in next st, sc in next st; rep from * around—18 sts.

Rnd 4: Working in BLO, sc in each st around.

Rnds 5–13: Working in both loops, sc in each st around.

Rnd 14: Working in BLO, *sc2tog, sc in next st; rep from * around—12 sts.

Rnd 15: Working in both loops, sl st in each st around.

Rnd 16: *Sc2tog, sc in next 2 sts; rep from * around—9 sts.

- Place last stitch on stitch marker to prevent unraveling. Stuff piece firmly with fiberfill, adding more fiberfill as needed as remaining rounds are worked.

Rnd 17: Sc in next 3 sts, sc2tog, sc in next 4 sts—8 sts.

Rnd 18: *Sc in next st, sc2tog, sc in next st; rep from * around—6 sts.

Rnd 19: [Sc2tog] around; join with sl st in first sc—3 sts.

- Fasten off, leaving a long tail. Weave tail through last round and pull gently to close.

Finishing:

- Cut a letter "K" or "M" from the felt and adhere to the bottle with craft glue.

pot

Cooking up some Spaghetti (page 78) or tossing some Salad (page 100)? This pot will come in handy. My favorite color is red, but choose any color you want. A matching lid will keep your AmiguruME Eats warm until you're ready to serve.

INSTRUCTIONS

Pot:

BASE:

Rnd 1: With A, make an adjustable ring, ch 1, 6 sc in ring. Pull tail to close ring—6 sts. Do not join at end of each round until instructed. Place marker at beginning of round and move marker up as each round is completed.

Rnd 2: 2 sc in each st around—12 sts.

Rnd 3: *2 sc in next st, sc in next st; rep from * around—18 sts.

Rnd 4: *Sc in next st, 2 sc in next st, sc in next st; rep from * around—24 sts.

Rnd 5: *Sc in next 3 sts, 2 sc in next st; rep from * around—30 sts.

Rnd 6: *Sc in next st, 2 sc in next st, sc in next 3 sts; rep from * around—36 sts.

Rnd 7: *Sc in next 5 sts, 2 sc in next st; rep from * around—42 sts.

Rnd 8: *Sc in next 3 sts, 2 sc in next st, sc in next 3 sts; rep from * around—48 sts.

Rnd 9: *Sc in next 6 sts, 2 sc in next st, sc in next st; rep from * around—54 sts.

SIDES:

Rnd 10: Working in BLO, sc in each st around.

Rnds 11–20: Working in both loops, sc in each st around.

Rnd 21: Working in BLO, sc in each st around; change color to B.

Rnds 22–31: Working in both loops, sc in each st around.

Rnd 32: Working in FLO, *sc2tog, sc in next 16 sts; rep from * around—51 sts.

Rnd 33: Working in both loops, *sc in next 8 sts, sc2tog, sc in next 7 sts; rep from * around—48 sts.

Rnd 34: *Sc in next 6 sts, sc2tog; rep from * around—42 sts.

Rnd 35: *Sc in next 3 sts, sc2tog, sc in next 2 sts; rep from * around—36 sts.

- Place last stitch on stitch marker to prevent unraveling. With Rnds 1–9 as a template, cut a circle of plastic canvas. Fit the plastic canvas into the base.

Rnd 36: *Sc in next 4 sts, sc2tog; rep from * around—30 sts.

Rnd 37: *Sc in next 2 sts, sc2tog, sc in next st; rep from * around—24 sts.

Rnd 38: *Sc in next 2 sts, sc2tog; rep from * around—18 sts.

Rnd 39: *Sc2tog, sc in next st; rep from * around—12 sts.

Rnd 40: [Sc2tog] around; join with sl st in first sc—6 sts.

- Fasten off, leaving a long tail. Weave tail through last round and pull gently to close. Weave in ends. Fold Rnds 32–36 down toward the inside of the pot. With matching yarn, sew around the inside edge to secure, being careful not to let the stitches show on the right side of the pot.

HANDLE (MAKE 2):

Rnd 1: With C, make an adjustable ring, ch 1, 6 sc in ring. Pull tail to close ring— 6 sts. Do not join at end of each round until instructed. Place marker at beginning of round and move marker up as each round is completed.

Rnd 2: 2 sc in each st around—12 sts.

Rnds 3–4: Sc in each st around; join with sl st in first sc at end of last rnd.

- Fasten off, leaving a long tail. Stuff each handle and sew to sides of pot.

Lid:

Rnds 1–9: Work same as Rnds 1–9 of pot.

Rnd 10: *Sc in next 4 sts, 2 sc in next st, sc in next 4 sts; rep from * around—60 sts.

Rnd 11: Working in BLO, *sc2tog, sc in next 8 sts; rep from * around—54 sts.

Rnd 12: Working in both loops, *sc in next 3 sts, sc2tog, sc in next 4 sts; rep from * around—48 sts.

Rnd 13: *Sc2tog, sc in next 6 sts; rep from * around— 42 sts.

Rnd 14: *Sc in next 2 sts, sc2tog, sc in next 3 sts; rep from * around—36 sts.

Skill Level:
EASY

MATERIALS AND TOOLS

Red worsted weight yarn (A) (4)

White worsted weight yarn (B) (4)

Black worsted weight yarn (C) (4)

Crochet hook: 3.25 mm (size D-3 U.S.)

Stitch marker

Yarn needle

Polyester fiberfill

Plastic canvas, 12 × 18 inches (30.5 × 45.5 cm)

STITCHES AND TECHNIQUES USED

Adjustable ring, page 11

Chain stitch (ch), page 9

Single crochet (sc), page 10

Back loops only (BLO), page 19

Change color, page 20

Front loops only (FLO), page 19

Single crochet two together (sc2tog), page 18

Slip stitch (sl st), page 10

Rnds 15–19: Work same as Rnds 36–40 of pot.

- Fasten off, leaving a long tail. Flatten lid, weave tail through last round, and pull gently to close. Sew through the layers of crocheted fabric to hold the flat shape of the lid, secure, and weave in ends.

KNOB:

Rnd 1: With C, make an adjustable ring, ch 1, 6 sc in ring. Pull tail to close ring—6 sts. Do not join at end of each round until instructed. Place marker at beginning of round and move marker up as each round is completed.

Rnd 2: 2 sc in each st around—12 sts.

Rnd 3: Working in BLO, sc in each st.

Rnd 4: Working in both loops, *sc2tog, sc in next 2 sts; rep from * around—9 sts.

Rnd 5: Sc in each st around; join with sl st in first sc.

- Fasten off, leaving a long tail. Stuff with fiberfill. Sew to the center of the lid. Weave in remaining ends.

frying pan & spatula

Skill Level:
EASY

If you want to fry an Egg (page 26) with some Bacon (page 28), or sauté Fish (page 88), you'll need a large pan like this one. Crochet the Spatula to go along with it for a power-cooking duo.

INSTRUCTIONS

Pan:

BASE:

Rnd 1: With A, make an adjustable ring, ch 1, 6 sc in ring. Pull tail to close ring—6 sts. Do not join at end of each round until instructed. Place marker at beginning of round and move marker up as each round is completed.

Rnd 2: 2 sc in each st around—12 sts.

Rnd 3: *2 sc in next st, sc in next st; rep from * around—18 sts.

Rnd 4: *Sc in next st, 2 sc in next st, sc in next st; rep from * around—24 sts.

Rnd 5: *Sc in next 3 sts, 2 sc in next st; rep from * around—30 sts.

Rnd 6: *Sc in next st, 2 sc in next st, sc in next 3 sts; rep from * around—36 sts.

MATERIALS AND TOOLS

Gray worsted weight yarn (A) **(4)**

Black worsted weight yarn (B) **(4)**

Crochet hook: 3.25 mm (size D-3 U.S.)

Stitch marker

Yarn needle

Plastic canvas sheet, 12 × 18 inches (30.5 cm × 45.5 cm)

STITCHES AND TECHNIQUES USED

Adjustable ring, page 11

Chain stitch (ch), page 9

Single crochet (sc), page 10

Back loops only (BLO), page 19

Single crochet two together (sc2tog), page 18

Slip stitch (sl st), page 10

Rnd 7: *Sc in next 5 sts, 2 sc in next st; rep from * around—42 sts.

Rnd 8: *Sc in next 3 sts, 2 sc in next st, sc in next 3 sts; rep from * around—48 sts.

Rnd 9: *Sc in next 6 sts, 2 sc in next st, sc in next st; rep from * around—54 sts.

Rnd 10: *Sc in next 5 sts, 2 sc in next st, sc in next 3 sts; rep from * around—60 sts.

Rnd 11: *2 sc in next st, sc in next 9 sts; rep from * around—66 sts.

Rnd 12: *Sc in next 5 sts, 2 sc in next st, sc in next 5 sts; rep from * around—72 sts.

SIDES:

Rnd 13: Working in BLO, sc in each st around Rnd 12.

Rnds 14–22: Working in both loops, sc in each st around.

Rnd 23: *Sc2tog, sc in next 22 sts; rep from * around—69 sts.

Rnd 24: *Sc in next 10 sts, sc2tog, sc in next 11 sts; rep from * around—66 sts.

Rnd 25: *Sc in next 4 sts, sc2tog, sc in next 5 sts; rep from * around—60 sts.

Rnd 26: *Sc2tog, sc in next 8 sts; rep from * around—54 sts.

Rnd 27: *Sc in next 5 sts, sc2tog, sc in next 2 sts; rep from * around—48 sts.

Rnd 28: *Sc in next 6 sts, sc2tog; rep from * around—42 sts.

Rnd 29: *Sc in next 2 sts, sc2tog, sc in next 3 sts; rep from * around—36 sts.

- Place last stitch on stitch marker to prevent unraveling. With Rnds 1–12 of the base as a template, cut a circle of plastic canvas. Place plastic canvas on the base. Hold the plastic canvas in place as you continue working the remaining rounds.

Rnd 30: *Sc2tog, sc in next 4 sts; rep from * around—30 sts.

Rnd 31: *Sc in next 2 sts, sc2tog, sc in next st; rep from * around—24 sts.

Rnd 32: *Sc2tog, sc in next 2 sts; rep from * around—18 sts.

Rnd 33: *Sc in next st, sc2tog; rep from * around—12 sts.

Rnd 34: [Sc2tog] around; join with sl st in first sc—6 sts.

- Fasten off, leaving a long tail. Weave the tail through the last round, pull gently to close, then weave through the base to hold the two pieces in place. Fold Rnds 13–22 to form the edge of the pan. With A, sew around the inside edge to secure.

HANDLE:

Rnd 1: With B, make an adjustable ring, ch 1, 6 sc in ring. Pull tail to close ring—6 sts. Do not join at end of each round until instructed. Place marker at beginning of round and move marker up as each round is completed.

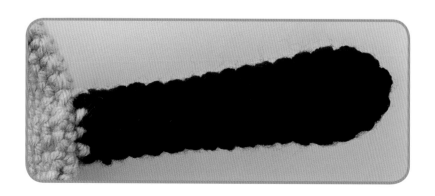

Rnd 2: 2 sc in each st around—12 sts.

Rnds 3 and 4: Sc in each st around.

Rnd 5: *Sc2tog, sc in next 4 sts; rep from * around—10 sts.

Rnds 6–9: Sc in each st around.

Rnd 10: *Sc2tog, sc in next 3 sts; rep from * around—8 sts.

Rnds 11–16: Sc in each st around; change color to A at end of last round.

Rnds 17–21: Sc in each st around; join with sl st in first sc at end of last round.

- Fasten off, leaving a long tail. Cut a piece of plastic canvas measuring 1 × 6 inches (2.5 × 15 cm) and insert in handle. Fold the handle and encased plastic canvas 1 inch (2.5 cm) from the end. Sew this 1-inch (2.5 cm) segment to the side of the pan. Weave in ends.

Spatula:

HANDLE:

Rnd 1: With B, make an adjustable ring, ch 1, 6 sc in ring. Pull tail to close ring— 6 sts. Do not join at end of each round until instructed.

Place marker at beginning of round and move marker up as each round is completed.

Rnd 2: 2 sc in each st around—12 sts.

Rnds 3–4: Sc in each st around.

Rnd 5: *Sc2tog, sc in next 4 sts; rep from * around—10 sts.

Rnds 6–9: Sc in each st around.

Rnd 10: *Sc2tog, sc in next 3 sts; rep from * around— 8 sts.

Rnd 11: Sc in each st around.

Rnd 12: Sl st in each st around; change color to B.

Rnds 13–14: Sc in each st around.

Rnd 15: Sc2tog, sc in each remaining st around—7 sts.

Rnds 16–30: Sc in each st around; join with sl st in first sc at end of last round.

- Fasten off, leaving a long tail. Cut a piece of plastic canvas measuring 1 × 7 inches (2.5 × 17.5 cm) and insert into the handle.

BLADE:

Rnd 1: With A, ch 7, sc in 2nd ch from hook and in next 4 chs, 3 sc in last ch; working in opposite side of foundation chain, sc in next 5

chs, 3 sc in beginning ch— 16 sts. Do not join at end of each round until instructed. Place marker at beginning of round and move marker up as each round is completed.

Rnd 2: Sc in next 6 sts, 2 sc in next st, sc in next 7 sts, 2 sc in next st, sc in next st—18 sts.

Rnds 3–10: Sc in each st around; join with sl st in first sc at end of last round.

- Fasten off, leaving a long tail. Cut a square of plastic canvas that is slightly smaller than the spatula and insert into the flattened spatula blade. With the end yarn tail, seam the stitches of Rnd 10 together. Overlap 1 inch (2.5 cm) of handle over the rest of spatula and sew in place. Weave in ends.

Finishing:

- With A, stitch 3 long, straight, black lines on each side of the spatula.

RESOURCES

YARNS

Bernat Satin; worsted weight yarn (4)

Cascade 220; worsted weight yarn (4)

Caron Simply Soft; worsted weight yarn (4)

I Love This Yarn; worsted weight yarn (4)

Lion Brand Vanna's Choice; worsted weight yarn (4)

Red Heart Soft; worsted weight yarn (4)

Red Heart Super Saver; worsted weight yarn (4)

I Love This Sport Yarn; lightweight yarn (3)

DMC Natura Just Cotton; fine weight yarn (2)

HOOKS

Clover Amour Crochet Hooks

Clover Soft Touch Hooks

POLYESTER FIBERFILL

Fairfield 100% Polyester Poly-fil

FELT

CPE Polyester Felt

Creatology Craft Felt

Kunin Eco-fi Felt

WAX MELTS

Aromabeads Wax Melts

ScentSationals Wax Cubes

Scentsy Wax Bar

Village Candle Wax Melts

WHERE TO BUY

Aromabeads
candlemart.com

Bernat/Caron Yarns
yarnspirations.com

DMC Embroidery Floss
dmc.com

Glass Eyes
glasseyesonline.com

Hobby Lobby
hobbylobby.com

Jo-ann Fabric and Craft Stores
joann.com

Lion Brand Yarn Company
lionbrand.com

Michaels
michaels.com

Red Heart Yarns
redheart.com

Scentsationals
Scentsationals.com

Scentsy
scentsy.com

Village Candle
villagecandle.com

ACKNOWLEDGMENTS

'd like to thank my editor, Elysia Liang, who took this project and ran with it. I don't know if I've ever worked with a more patient person! I appreciate your valuable insight, creative nudges, and fun ideas to get the book going where I wanted. Thanks to my tech editor, Randy Cavaliere, photographer Chris Bain, whose pictures made me squeal with delight, and the rest of the book team: Scott Amerman, Shannon Plunkett, Lorie Pagnozzi, and Ellen Day Hudson.

Thanks to Kate McKean, my agent, who saw me through this process once again and constantly has my back when I need it.

Thanks to my supportive hubby, Paul, who got a new grill (I could have crocheted you one) and cooked all the dinners while I was writing this book. Also to my three boys, who let their mom crochet and write while they behaved like angels. Maybe someday one of you will want to crochet? Maybe? I love all four of you so so much. Thanks to my mom and sisters, always supportive with an "OMG that's so cute!" on the group text in response to my dozens of crocheted food photos. Really, I do love to hear it. Mom, thanks for giving me the crafty gene. My in-laws, thanks for being actually really great in-laws who love to hear about the crochet escapades I get myself into and who are always willing to help.

Last, thanks to my online CraftyisCool.com fans. Without social media I don't think I'd be doing this for a living, so let me give you a giant cyberhug. Thanks for following me on Facebook, Twitter, and Instagram, and whatever comes next.

ABOUT THE AUTHOR

ALLISON HOFFMAN has always been a crafty person, but when she found crocheting she never looked back. She started writing and designing patterns on her website, CraftyisCool.com, in 2007. She has since designed for magazines, art exhibits, and movies. Her work has been featured on Netflix, *The Martha Stewart Show*, *Late Night with Seth Meyers*, *The Today Show*, *Glee*, *Yo Gabba Gabba*, *Conan*, and more. She can usually be found next to her yarn wall, crocheting and watching true-crime TV shows. She is the author of *AmiguruME* and *AmiguruME Pets*, published by Sterling Publishing. *AmiguruME Eats* is her third amigurumi book, and she thinks it's the tastiest one yet.

INDEX